"I can think of few things that the contempor[...] much as the ancient practice of lectio divina. In [...] by which we are to receive Scripture. The focus [...] biblical text itself, and the commentary and questions push us back to the text to listen for God's address. My hope is that this well-written and accessible tool will assist readers in the practice of lectio divina."

—**Craig Bartholomew**, coauthor, *The Drama of Scripture*

"Stephen Binz has done an admirable job of introducing his readers to the process of lectio divina and immersing them in it. Through teaching the practice of this ancient way of studying the Bible, this series of Scripture studies will recharge and deepen the faith and lives of many, who thereafter will use the art for private devotions and/or in small groups. I heartily recommend this series to individuals and churches who want to join in the spirited revival of Christianity in our time!"

—**Marva J. Dawn**, Regent College

"At their recent Synod the world's Catholic bishops recommended lectio divina to all Christ's disciples, for prayerfully reading and making God's Word one's spiritual nourishment follows well-trod paths in the Christian tradition. Stephen Binz guides us on these paths in his Ancient-Future Bible Study series. I am pleased to recommend this project with enthusiasm."

—**Terrence Prendergast, SJ**, Archbishop of Ottawa

"Lectio divina, despite its centuries-long use, is still little known outside of monastic and academic settings. Ancient-Future Bible Study, a project that does great credit to Brazos Press, has in mind to correct that historical defect in Christian piety."

—**Patrick Henry Reardon**, author, *Creation and the Patriarchal Histories*

"Ancient-Future Bible Study brings a centuries-old approach to Scripture and prayer into the twenty-first century, providing sound commentary, thoughtful insights, and meaningful suggestions for personal reflection and meditation. Stephen Binz invites us to open our minds and hearts to the transforming power of God's Word. Under his guidance, the wisdom of the Bible comes vividly to life."

—**Carl McColman**, author, *The Big Book of Christian Mysticism*

"Stephen Binz has a knack for popularizing the Bible. His latest series, Ancient-Future Bible Study, demonstrates once more his ability to give people sound guidance as they read the Bible. I am happy to warmly recommend this modern application of the ancient method of lectio divina—the once and future way to read the Bible prayerfully—centered on fascinating characters from the Old and New Testaments."

—**Fr. Ronald D. Witherup**, author, *The Bible Companion*

"A method of Bible study that has a long and celebrated history in the church is given renewed momentum with this series. The goal here is more than instruction. The five movements of lectio divina are an invitation to immerse oneself in the riches of our biblical tradition and to give flesh to that tradition in our daily lives. This series will be a wonderful aid for the development of one's spiritual life."

—**Dianne Bergant, CSA**, Catholic Theological Union

"This series is a wonderful gift for the church in late modernity. In an era of twittered attention, we have inculcated all sorts of bad reading habits that we then bring to Scripture. The Ancient-Future Bible Study prescribes a counter-formative regimen: the personal and communal practice of lectio divina or 'sacred reading.' For some this will be a strange, new practice; but it will quickly feel as natural as breathing. So find some friends, take up this series, and read anew!"

—**James K. A. Smith**, Calvin College; author, *Desiring the Kingdom: Worship, Worldview, and Cultural Formation*

"Stephen Binz's new series allows us to put down the commentaries and word studies and let the beautiful poignancy of the text seep into our souls, all with the aid of the Holy Spirit. I heartily recommend it."

—**Tony Jones**, Solomon's Porch, Minneapolis; author, *The New Christians: Dispatches from the Emergent Frontier*

"Stephen Binz, a responsible biblical scholar and experienced pastor, has undertaken the important project of leading non-professional but committed readers of the Bible into a spiritually enlivening encounter with the biblical text through engagement with some of the fascinating characters who people its pages. Anyone yearning to pray the biblical text will find this series a useful companion."

—**Sandra M. Schneiders**, Jesuit School of Theology

ΔNCIENT-FUTURE BIBLE STUDY

WOMEN
OF THE
TORAH

Matriarchs and Heroes of Israel

STEPHEN J. BINZ

Brazos Press
a division of Baker Publishing Group
Grand Rapids, Michigan

© 2011 by Stephen J. Binz

Published by Brazos Press
a division of Baker Publishing Group
P.O. Box 6287, Grand Rapids, MI 49516-6287
www.brazospress.com

Printed in the United States of America

Library of Congress Cataloging-in-Publication Data

Binz, Stephen J., 1955–
     Women of the Torah : matriarchs and heroes of Israel / Stephen J. Binz.
          p.   cm. — (Ancient-future Bible study)
     ISBN 978-1-58743-281-1 (pbk.)
     1. Women in the Bible. 2. Bible. O.T. Genesis—Criticism, interpretation, etc. 3. Devotional literature. I. Title.
BS575.B56 2011
221.8′3054—dc22   2010028529

Some content from "Welcome to Ancient-Future Bible Study" originally appeared in Stephen J. Binz, *Conversing with God in Scripture: A Contemporary Approach to Lectio Divina* (Ijamsville, MD: The Word Among Us Press, 2008).

11   12   13   14   15   16   17   7   6   5   4   3   2   1

Contents

Acknowledgments

For the past several years my work has focused on making connections between ancient practices and contemporary experiences. My speaking, writing, and counseling under the trademark Bridge-Building Opportunities has emphasized the link between past and present, East and West, time-honored tradition and progressive renewal in the fields of biblical theology, Christian spirituality, and personal growth.

When I discovered the mission of Brazos Press, I felt that I had found a new home. By its own definition, Brazos Press is "staked on the discernment that while various existing Christian categories (liberal and conservative, mainline and evangelical, even Catholic and Protestant) prove increasingly unserviceable, there is at the same time occurring a robust renewal of classical, orthodox Christianity across many of the old lines or borders." This is a publisher that is eager to cross boundaries, build bridges, and extend the vital roots of the ancient Christian tradition into the twenty-first century.

I am grateful to Jim Kinney, associate publisher and editorial director of Baker Academic and Brazos Press, for supporting my work. Lisa Ann Cockrel, editor for this series, has masterfully guided these books through the editorial process and improved this work with her many ideas. I also appreciate the skillful work of Lisa Beth Anderson, Rodney Clapp, Steve Ayers, BJ Heyboer, Jeremy Wells, Caitlin Mackenzie, and the whole Brazos team for their efforts to refine and promote this project.

The term "Ancient-Future" seems to perfectly express the bridge between ancient wisdom and future possibilities that I want to create in this series. The term is applied in a number of other spheres to emphasize a blending of tradition and innovation. In the arts, ancient-future music and dance is created through fusing centuries-old traditions with contemporary genres and technology. By learning from the world's great traditions and ancient practices, artists create cross-cultural expressions that are richly profound yet also widely appealing.

I am particularly indebted to the work of the late Robert Webber, many of whose books use the term "Ancient-Future" to express his mission of drawing wisdom from the past and translating those insights into the present and future life of the church, its faith, worship, ministry, and spirituality. In his own words: "My argument is that the era of the early church (AD 100–500), and particularly the second century, contains insights which evangelicals need to recover." This series resonates with his outstanding work and hopefully, in some small way, will honor his memory and continue his vision.

Finally, I am grateful to all my friends and colleagues in the field of biblical studies and to all pastors, lay ministers, and church volunteers who are dedicated to an anciently rooted and forward-looking Christianity. Particularly I want to express my appreciation to my wife Pamela, a professor of music, for the loving support and inspiration she constantly offers to me.

Welcome to Ancient-Future Bible Study

Ancient-Future Bible Study unites contemporary study of the Bible with an experience of the church's most ancient way of reading Scripture, *lectio divina*. By combining the old and the new in a fertile synthesis, this study helps modern people encounter the *sacra pagina*, the inspired text, as God intends it for the church. Through solid historical and literary study and the time-honored practice of lectio divina, the mind and the heart are brought into an experience of God through a careful and prayerful reading of the biblical texts.

As the Word of its divine author, the Bible is not just a literary anthology of ancient texts; it is inspired literature addressed to God's people. God intends the sacred texts to move from our heads to the depths of our hearts and to form us as a new people living in God's reign. Ancient-Future Bible Study guides readers to listen to Scripture within the tradition and scholarship of the church in order to unleash its life-changing potential.

The ancient art of lectio divina is rooted in the Jewish tradition of Jesus, and it was nourished through the desert spirituality of the early centuries, the patristic writers of the ancient church, and the monastic tradition through the ages. In our day, lectio divina is experiencing a worldwide revival as Christians are returning to age-old wisdom to experience the Scriptures in a deeper and more complete way.

As you experience Ancient-Future Bible Study, you will realize how the church's long tradition of biblical study, reflection, prayer, discernment, and contemplative action can enrich your discipleship. You will learn how to dispose yourself to be formed by the Word of God as you join with the array of men and women through the ages whose lives have been transformed by that same living Word.

Reasons for Studying the Bible

Most often people study the Bible for one of three reasons. First, they study for information and knowledge. This usually includes a search for historical facts, doctrinal truths, and moral guidance. Second, they study to find advice for solving a personal need or getting through a life crisis. This usually involves seeking out lists of specific passages that speak to the particular needs of the moment. Third, they study so they can defend their faith and witness to others. This usually consists of choosing selected passages to remember and quote, so they can argue for a particular approach to faith or help lead others toward the truth. While all of these objectives can lead to good results, their accomplishments are always limited and partial.

The most complete reason for studying Scripture is for the purpose of encountering the living God through the sacred text. This divine encounter leads not just to more information and advice but to a deeply rooted transformation of life. The inspired Word evokes a spiritual transformation within the lives of those who allow God's Word to do its true work, urging us to personal growth in Christ and fuller discipleship.

For Scripture to have its deepest effects in us we must approach the text with humility, reverence, and expectation. As we receive its revelation and understand its truth, Scripture has the ability to gradually change our minds and mold our hearts. Unlike any other literature, the words of the Bible can renew our lives when we approach the text as an encounter with its divine author.

The Indwelling of the Holy Spirit

The Bible was written under the inspiration of the Holy Spirit. God's "breathing in," acting in union with the human authors of the texts, makes the Scriptures the Word of the living God. Because God is the primary author of the Bible, we can be assured that the texts have a power that transcends that of any other spiritual reading.

God's inspiration of the biblical books does not refer only to a past reality, to the historical time in which the biblical authors were guided to write the texts. Rather, the work of God's Spirit is an ongoing reality within the inspired books. The sacred texts remain inspired; they are forever permeated with divine breath and are filled now with the Spirit of God.

This understanding of the Spirit's enduring and ongoing presence in the biblical texts is the foundation of lectio divina. Through the Holy Spirit, God addresses his Word to us here and now through the ancient text. Because of the indwelling Spirit, the Word is alive and has the power to transform us. The Word of God is charged with creative power to change and renew us from within.

The Movements of Lectio Divina

Lectio divina (LEK-tsee-oh dih-VEEN-ah) is best translated, though incompletely, as "sacred reading." Its revitalization, like the renewal of other spiritual practices from the early church, is becoming a means of deep spiritual growth for people today. Lectio divina helps us return to the most ancient understanding of the sacredness of the inspired text. The Bible is not like a textbook, used for looking up factual documentation, nor is it like a manual, describing a how-to method for solving problems. Rather, it is a means of forming our life in God and joining us to the story of God's people.

The process of lectio divina appeals not only to our minds but also to our imaginations and feelings. We seek to understand and experience Scripture as a real communication, as God personally addressing us. In practicing lectio divina, we get caught up in the literature and learn to love the text itself; we read it reflectively, lingering over it, and let it reach the depths of our hearts. We let go of our own agenda and expectations, gradually opening ourselves to what God wants us to experience through the sacred page.

There is no single method for the practice of lectio divina. It is not a rigid step-by-step system for encountering God in biblical passages. The spiritual masters of the early church distrusted methods of prayer and spiritual practice that were too rigidly defined, wishing instead to cultivate the freedom necessary to respond to the Spirit's promptings. Lectio divina aims toward a holistic experience of Scripture, incorporating our intellects, feelings, and actions.

Ancient-Future Bible Study incorporates five "movements." Comparable to the movements in a classical work of music, each movement has its own characteristics and can even be practiced independently of the others. There is plenty of room for personal interpretation within the tradition. Individually and together, lectio, meditatio, oratio, contemplatio, and operatio contribute to the full experience of lectio divina.

Pronunciation Guide

Lectio—LEK-tsee-oh
Meditatio—meh-dih-TAH-tsee-oh
Oratio—oh-RAH-tsee-oh
Contemplatio—con-tem-PLAH-tsee-oh
Operatio—oh-peh-RAH-tsee-oh

Lectio—*Reading the Text with a Listening Ear*

Lectio is more than ordinary reading. It might best be described as listening deeply—what St. Benedict in the sixth century described as hearing "with the ear of our heart." This listening requires that we try to receive God's Word with as little prejudgment as possible, as if we were hearing it for the first time. Lectio urges us to create a space within us for the new wisdom and understanding God wants to give us through the sacred page.

Saint Ambrose in the fourth century urged readers to avoid the tendency to read large passages in haste: "We should read not in agitation, but in calm; not hurriedly, but slowly, a few words at a time, pausing in attentive reflection. . . . Then the readers will experience their ability to enkindle the ardor of prayer." We might even consider returning to the ancient practice of reading texts aloud in order to instill within ourselves the sense of reading Scripture as a deep listening.

The essential question to ask in this first movement is, "What does the text say and what does it mean?" The Jewish rabbis and the church's patristic writers show us that there is no clear distinction between studying and praying Scripture. The more we come to understand the text with our minds, the more we are capable of being changed by the text. Wrestling with the text and seeking to comprehend its meaning is an important part of encountering God there and being changed by that encounter.

Once we've read the text slowly and carefully, Ancient-Future Bible Study invites us to learn from the commentary that follows the biblical passage. This too is part of listening to the text, only here we listen with the understanding of the church and with some basic insights of biblical scholarship. This listening to the text, with its multiple layers of meaning and rich history of interpretation, forms the foundation on which we experience the subsequent movements of lectio divina. We do what we can to make sure our reading of the text is faithful and true, so that we don't reduce God's revelation to our own imaginary constructions. On this firm basis, we construct the process of prayerfully encountering God's Word.

We might read the text as literature, looking at its words, metaphors, images, and characters. We could look at its structure and its literary form— is it poetry, parable, history, proverb, legal code, epic, or apocalypse? We should realize that God's truth is expressed in a variety of types of literature, each type expressing truth in a different way. The more we can comprehend something of the original historical, cultural, literary, and religious context of the passage, the better we will be able to probe all the potential the text can offer us.

In lectio, the words of Scripture become the means of God speaking to us. As God's Spirit guided the human authors to express the truth that God wished to entrust to the Scriptures, God also guides us through that same Spirit as we read the Bible as God's Word to us.

Meditatio—*Reflecting on the Meaning and Message of the Text*

The question to ask in this movement is, "What does the text say to me and mean to me?" Meditatio aims to bring the biblical passage into the sphere of my own life as I seek to understand how the Scripture passage speaks to me today.

Though there is a wide gap of time, language, and culture between the world of the biblical writers and our own world, meditatio bridges that gap. By reflecting on the text as well as on our own experiences, thoughts, challenges, and questions, we can grow in our understanding that God is speaking personally to us through the scriptural text. This reflection forms connections between the text of yesterday and the today of our lives.

Ancient-Future Bible Study stimulates meditatio through the use of questions for reflection. These questions encourage a deeper and more personal consideration of the text. They challenge the reader to create a dialogue between the ancient text and life today. As the Word of God, the Bible has a richness of meaning that can be discovered in every age and every culture. It has a particular message that can be received by everyone who listens to God's Word in the context of daily experiences and in the same Spirit in which it was written.

The more we meditate on God's Word, the more it seeps into our lives and saturates our thoughts and feelings. Meditatio allows the dynamic Word of God to so penetrate our lives that it truly infuses our minds and hearts and we begin to embody its truth and its goodness.

Oratio—*Praying in Response to God's Word*

Careful lectio and reflective meditatio open the way for God to enter into our hearts and inflame them with the grace of his love. There, at the core of our being, we naturally want to respond to the One whose voice we have heard. Oratio is our prayerful response to God's Word.

Lectio divina is fundamentally a dialogue with God, a gentle oscillation between listening to God and responding to him in prayer. When we recognize that God has offered us a message that is unique to our own lives—an insight, a challenge, a comfort, a call—we arrive at the moment when we must ask ourselves, "Now what am I going to say in response to God?" This is the moment of prayer.

Oratio is not just any form of prayer. It is born from the experience of listening to God in Scripture. The biblical words we have heard and reflected on become the words of our prayer. The style and vocabulary of our prayer are enriched through the inspired words of the biblical tradition. Whether our oratio is an act of praise or thanksgiving, of petition or repentance, we pray in response to what we have heard. Our prayers no longer consist of mechanically repeated formulas. Rather, they resonate with the faith, hope, and love that animated the people of the Bible in their journey with God.

Ancient-Future Bible Study offers examples of this type of prayer. After each session of lectio and meditatio, we are encouraged to continue in intimate prayer to God, melding the words, images, and sentiments of the biblical text with personal thoughts, feelings, and desires arising from the heart.

Contemplatio—*Quietly Resting in God*

Both oratio and contemplatio are forms of prayer. Oratio is our active, word-filled prayer in response to God's Word. Contemplatio is prayer without words. It is the response to God that remains after words are no longer necessary or helpful. It is simply enjoying the experience of quietly being in God's presence.

Contemplatio requires that we let go of any effort to be in charge of the process. When we feel God drawing us into a deeper awareness of his divine presence, we gradually abandon our intellectual activity and let ourselves be wooed into God's embrace. We no longer have to think or reason, listen or speak. The experience resembles that of lovers holding each other in wordless silence or of a sleeping child resting in the arms of his or her mother.

Though we may think the movement of contemplatio is passive and uneventful, it is not. When we humbly expose our heart, the center of our being, to God, what happens within us during those moments is really not up to us. In contrast to the rapid, noisy communication of our technological world, quiet, receptive stillness is the atmosphere in which the most important communication occurs. God's grace is truly at work in those moments, and the Holy Spirit is changing us without our direct knowledge or understanding.

Operatio—*Faithful Witness in Daily Life*

After reading, reflecting, and praying over a scriptural passage, we should be impacted in a way that makes a difference in our daily lives. Operatio is our lived response to the biblical text. The question operatio calls forth from us is, "How can I live out the Word of God that I have heard in my heart?"

We cannot prayerfully read Scripture without being changed in some specific way. As we deepen our relationship with God through the movements of lectio divina, our actions become vehicles of his presence to others. We become channels of God's compassion and mercy, becoming "doers of the word, and not merely hearers" (James 1:22), bringing about God's loving purposes in our daily lives.

Contemplatio and operatio should not be totally distinct and separate. Their impulses grow together in the heart of one who prayerfully reads Scripture. Contemplatio does not separate us from the world, and operatio is not genuine unless it grows out of contemplative reflection. Apart from contemplatio, operatio could become superficial pragmatism.

The Bible should never be viewed as simply a collection of maxims to be put into practice. Rarely does Scripture offer us concrete details about what to do in specific situations. Our human reason and experience must always accompany our prayerful discernment as we decide how to live out the Word of God. Listening, reflection, prayer, and contemplation are all necessary components from which flows the operatio of Christian discipleship. Lectio divina helps us become contemplative activists and active contemplatives.

The Essence of Lectio Divina

The movements of lectio divina are more like the colors of a rainbow than clearly defined stages. They overlap, blending into one another, ebbing and flowing according to the rhythm of the divine Spirit and the human heart. The five movements used in Ancient-Future Bible Study are part of a rich tradition, though additional phases are sometimes found in other historical forms of the practice: studium (study), cogitatio (reflection), consolatio (comfort), discretio (discernment), deliberatio (decision making), compassio (compassion), and actio (action).

While the most ancient practice of lectio divina is not a rigid system of biblical reflection, nor does its method require any particular steps, there are a few characteristics that identify the authentic practice of lectio divina:

✝ *Lectio divina is a personal encounter with God through Scripture.* The text itself is a gateway to God. Through the inspired Scripture, we meet the God who loves us and desires our response.

✢ *Lectio divina establishes a dialogue between the reader of Scripture and God.* The attentive reader listens to God through the text and responds to God in heartfelt prayer. The heart of lectio divina is this gentle conversation with God.

✢ *Lectio divina creates a heart-to-heart intimacy with God.* In the Bible, the heart is a person's innermost core, the place from which one's deepest longings, motivations, decisions, memories, and desires arise. The prayerful reader responds to God's Word with the whole heart and thereby grows in a relationship with God at the deepest level of intimacy.

✢ *Lectio divina leads to contemplation and action.* There is a moment in all true love that leads to a level of communication too deep for words. Prayerful reading inevitably leads to that deepest form of communication with God, which is loving silence. In addition, all true love must be expressed in action. Eventually words become inadequate, and love must be demonstrated in deeds arising from a changed heart.

The Word of God and its power to change us are gifts from God that we must accept into our lives. In order to receive the gift of divine intimacy, we must create the necessary conditions within us. Openheartedness, faithfulness, and expectation will enable us to more readily listen and receive. The more we remove the obstacles in the way—our inner resistance, our fear of intimacy, our impatient awareness of time, our desire to control the process, and our self-concern—the more we can expect Scripture to transform our lives.

Sometimes the changes are remarkable; more often they are subtle. We gradually become aware that the fruit of studying the Bible is the fruit of the Spirit: "love, joy, peace, patience, kindness, generosity, faithfulness, gentleness, and self-control" (Gal. 5:22–23). When we begin to notice this fruit in the way we live each day, we will know that the Word of God is working within us.

Your Personal Practice of Ancient-Future Bible Study

✢ This study is designed to provide maximum flexibility so that you can make lectio divina a regular part of your life according to your circumstances. If you are able to make the time in your daily schedule, you will want to reflect on one chapter each day. If not, you may select three weekdays to read three chapters per week. Or if your weekends are more leisurely, you may choose to reflect on two chapters per weekend.

‡ Reading Plan #1—30 days/5 weeks
  • Engage six lessons per week

‡ Reading Plan #2—60 days/10 weeks
  • Engage three lessons per week

‡ Reading Plan #3—90 days/15 weeks
  • Engage two lessons per weekend

‡ Whatever pace you choose for your practice of lectio divina, try to find a regular time during the day that can become a pattern for you. Choose a quiet and comfortable place where you will be undisturbed during the time of your lectio divina.

‡ During your regular time for lectio divina, try to rid yourself of as many distractions as possible. Before you begin reading the Bible, take time to call upon the Holy Spirit for guidance. Light a candle, ring a chime, kiss the Bible, or do some other action that will designate these moments as sacred time.

‡ Read the biblical text slowly and carefully. Read the passage in another translation, if you wish, to help your understanding. Don't hesitate to mark up this book with highlights, underlining, circles, or whatever will help you pay attention and remember the text and commentary.

‡ Follow the movements of lectio divina outlined in each section. Realize that this is only a tentative guide for the more important movements of God's Spirit within you. Write out your responses to the questions provided. The questions following the lectio are objective questions synthesizing your reading of the text and commentary. Those under meditatio are more personal questions, requiring thoughtful reflection. Try also to write comments on the sections of oratio, contemplatio, and operatio, according to the suggestions provided. The very act of writ-

ing will help you clarify your thoughts, bring new insights, and amplify your understanding.

✢ Approach your lectio divina with expectancy, trusting that God will indeed work deeply within you through his Word. Through this experience, know that you are placing yourself within a long procession of God's people through the ages who have allowed themselves to be transformed through lectio divina.

✢ Finally, try to be accountable to at least one other person for your regular practice of lectio divina. Tell a spouse, friend, spiritual director, or minister about your experience in order to receive their encouragement and affirmation.

Bringing Ancient-Future Bible Study to Churches

Throughout the history of salvation, God's Word has been directed first and foremost to a community, not just to individuals. The people of Israel, the community of disciples, and the early church were the recipients of God's self-communication expressed in the Scriptures. For this reason, studying the Bible in the context of a community of faith can deepen and enrich our individual experience.

Churches and other faith communities may choose to adopt Ancient-Future Bible Study and encourage its use in a variety of ways. Since this Bible study is ideally suited both for personal use by individuals and for communal practice, congregations are able to respect the many ways people desire to make Scripture a priority in their lives. By encouraging an array of options for participation, churches will increase the number of people in the congregation who are making reading and reflection on the Bible a regular part of their lives in Christ.

Collatio—The Communal Practice of Lectio Divina

The ancient term for the communal practice of lectio divina is collatio (coh-LAH-tsee-oh), a term that originally meant "a bringing together, interchange, or discussion." Its aim is building up a spiritual community around the Word of God. Collatio began in an age when books were rare and precious. Today, when everyone may have their own Bible, collatio may be practiced in many different ways.

Here are some ways of building up a faith community with Ancient-Future Bible Study:

‡ Offer this study to people who want to participate only on their own. Respect the fact that many people don't have the time or desire to gather with others. Instead they can be encouraged to read and reflect on their own with the prayerful support of the whole community.

‡ Promote the formation of informal groups made up of family, friends, neighbors, or work associates.

‡ Facilitate usage of the study through online communities or social networks. Online group members might want to commit themselves to sending an email or text message to the group offering their insights after reflecting on each Scripture passage.

‡ Set up small groups that meet regularly at church facilities or in homes. These groups may meet at different times throughout the week to offer convenient options for people in different circumstances. Groups could be made up of people with obvious connections: young adults, retired seniors, parents with young children, professionals, couples, etc. These groupings may encourage a deeper level of personal reflection among members.

Biblical reading and reflection on a regular basis is an important part of Christian discipleship. Every member of our congregations should be encouraged to make Bible reading and reflection a regular part of their lives. This is best accomplished when pastoral leadership promotes this practice and when people are personally invited to participate. When practicing lectio divina within a community of faith, we learn to place our own lives into the story of God's people throughout the ages.

Further Help for Groups

‡ Additional information for facilitating small groups with Ancient-Future Bible Study may be found starting on page 161 of this book.

‡ Since Ancient-Future Bible Study is divided into units of six lessons, motivated groups may choose to study five lessons per week on their own, with a weekly group session discussing insights from the daily lessons and practicing the sixth lesson of the week in the group.

‡ Groups with less daily time to study may divide the six lessons in half, choosing to study two lessons per week on their own, with a weekly group session discussing insights from the daily lessons and practicing the third lesson of the week in the group.

‡ The practice of lectio divina for each lesson will take about thirty minutes for an individual. Those who wish to spend extended time in reflection and prayer should allow for more time. The group session, using the suggestions at the back of this book, will take about ninety minutes.

‡ Additional information about Ancient-Future Bible Study, with descriptions of published and upcoming studies, may be found online at www .brazospress.com/ancientfuturebiblestudy. You can also connect to the series and its author on Facebook.

Introduction to *Women of the Torah: Matriarchs and Heroes of Israel*

People love stories. We beg for them as children; we delight in telling them as adults. Families love to hear and tell stories of origin, tales that often go back several generations. These stories may include narratives of immigration, difficult journeys, meeting spouses and falling in love. They may be sagas of struggles, surprises, suffering, fortune, and inevitably death of loved ones.

Stories are powerful media. They offer us identity and a personal history. Stories of ancestors keep them alive in our memory and perpetuate family traditions. Heroic stories, conversion stories, survival stories, and stories of faith all have the power to transform us and shape our lives.

The life of each one of us, with all its ups and downs, routines and wonders, is merely a discontinuous string of incidents until we create the narrative that gives them meaning. By creating the story, by writing the story in our own minds and telling it to others, we bring a coherent shape and meaning to our experiences and draw understanding from them. By weaving our experiences into a story, into a narrative of words and images, we shape the underlying themes of our lives into a meaningful form.

When people carry around a version of their story that doesn't serve their life and their future, often they are able to turn their story a bit so that another facet comes into view. For example, if your life story leaves you hopeless, feeling that all the troubles you have suffered and obstacles you have faced are a form of needless punishment, the narrative of your life leaves you with only a frustrated sadness. But if you could reconsider your personal narrative in light of other people who have struggled in similar ways and found positive meaning in their struggles, maybe you could grow to consider the difficulties of your life as a chance to cultivate resilience, a way to prepare for the unique challenges and tasks you could fulfill. By bringing new meaning to the events of our lives, we can shape our lives anew and tell a story that provides hope for the future. How we choose to frame our lives makes a huge difference in the way we live them.

The Bible is essentially the story of God in relationship to the world, a grand narrative made up largely of smaller stories of individual people, families, clans, and nations in relationship to God. The tellers of these sagas through the ages have shaped them into the story of God, and the literary artists who wrote the Scriptures formed these many little stories of God's people into the defining narrative of God and his people.

The women of the Torah, whose stories are told in this book, would probably be astonished to know that, thousands of years later, in a world they couldn't possibly imagine, people are still telling their stories. Their lives, like our own, were occupied with everyday activities. They ground grain, spun thread from raw wool, washed clothes with water from the well, kneaded and baked bread, and preserved fruits and meat for storage. They couldn't see how their own lives fit into the big picture of God's purposes in the world. Yet, they did catch glimpses of God at work, reflect on the meaning of their life events in light of the covenant, and tell their stories to their children and grandchildren. Because others passed on the episodes and repeated the words, their stories were treasured through the centuries—each a small patch stitched into the narrative quilt of God's people.

Even though the matriarch's stories are thousands of years old, and told about a world very different from our own, they still have the power to stir us, surprise us, captivate us, shock us, and throw a clarifying light on our own lives. Woven in and through the lives and stories of these women of the Torah are profound insights into the very heart of life. God is the constant presence whose breath animates the lives lived out in the pages of Scripture. It is God's grand narrative into which each of these tales fits, each colorful story with its own unpredictable structure and unexpected shape.

When we place our own story in dialogue with the biblical narrative, we continually renew our understanding of life and its meaning. We realize that our life is much larger than the sum of its parts, and we continually reshape our own story within the context of the defining narrative of God's saving history. Through reflective and prayerful listening to God's inspired Word, we gain the ongoing ability to refresh the meaning of our life as it unfolds. Though the biblical text is fixed and unchanging, it is kept alive and fresh for us as we reflect on its stories in the context of our own personal narratives. God's grand narrative is ongoing and includes the lives of each of us today. Our lives too fit into the story of this great God who does the unpredictable, sides with the lowly, ignores the obvious, turns our expectations upside down, and blesses the efforts of those who trust.

Questions to Consider

‡ Do I know someone whose story has brought me strength or wisdom? Who?

‡ In what way do I expect to better understand the meaning of my life through dialoguing with the stories of these biblical women?

Everyday Life for Women of the Torah

In the ancient world of the Bible, women did not have the same advantages and social privileges as men. In this patriarchal culture, a woman was dependent on her father for support before marriage and then on her husband after marriage. A woman was given as a wife to whomever her father desired. A woman's primary responsibility was to bear children for her husband. Property was inherited by sons rather than daughters, and women were mentioned in biblical genealogies only as exceptions to the rule. They had little legal power, were required to be virgins in order to be given in marriage, and were not allowed to divorce their husbands.

The emphasis on women's maternal roles derived from economic necessity. Women in ancient times needed to produce many children in order to contribute to the family labor supply and as a hedge against child mortality. Childbearing was rewarded with security and prestige. In this family-centered economy, women spent large amounts of time in activities related to childbirth and infant nurturing. To this primary work were added the tasks of household management, cleaning and washing, clothing the family by spinning, weaving, and sewing, and the instruction of children. This work within the family accounted for women's highest personal and social reward. The bitterest deprivation for a woman was barrenness, and widowhood without a father or son to care for her was a woman's most desperate state.

Because women in the Torah were subordinate to men in power and rights, those whose stories stand out most are often women who display unusual courage and resourcefulness in rising above their conventional roles. We remember how Rebekah's cleverness helped her obtain her husband's blessing for Jacob, her younger and favorite son. We recall how the mother and sister of Moses conspired together to save the life of Moses from the powerful decree of Egypt's king. We are encouraged by the persistence of the five daughters of Zelophehad as they insisted on their inheritance rights when their father died without sons.

Though women seem to be subordinate figures in the ancient world of the Bible, they play essential roles in the narratives of Israel's faith. Their roles in the literature, especially in family sagas, are far more influential, complex, and forceful than their legal status suggests. It is remarkable how many stories of women are found in the Bible's opening books and how thoroughly women determine the course of their people's early history. The names of Sarah, Rebekah, Rachel, and Miriam are essential to the telling of the Torah. The biblical authors write with great sensitivity about the details of life important to women. The stories of women often contrast the conventional norms of the culture with the respect and compassion God shows to women. They present a God who takes the side of women, rescuing them from abandonment, barrenness, and oppression, and assuring them of a noble destiny.

Questions to Consider

‡ What would I consider the most significant difference between the lives of women in ancient times and the lives of women today?

‡ Why would women have a greater role in Israel's religious literature than their legal power or social influence might suggest?

The Broad Spectrum of Women in the Torah

The Torah opens with a radical understanding of humanity that colors all the portrayals of men and women throughout the first five books of the Bible: male and female are made in the image of God (Gen. 1:27). This awareness provides a vision of humanity that is gender neutral, where man and woman are equal in forming the image of God. In the context of the ancient world, where in fact men were powerful and women subordinate, this basic insight of gender equality allows God's people to recognize that women may be subordinate in power without being inferior in essence.

This understanding had deep effects on the way Israel viewed itself. Though they were always small and vulnerable in comparison to the empires that surrounded them, their understanding of women allowed them to see their own history as honored by God, even though they were often overpowered and defeated by other peoples. In fact, Israel came to see itself as God's bride and spouse, a self-image that allowed the Israelites to see their noble purpose and look toward their glorious destiny.

Abraham cannot bring the divine promises to fulfillment without Sarah. She is just as much God's addressee and the bearer of the promises as her husband. She is the one from whom the promised son would be born. Over and over, God rescues Sarah and restores her to her rightful place. Yet, when Sarah becomes the oppressor of her servant Hagar, God stands on the side of the weakest, and he makes Hagar too a bearer of promises.

Rebekah makes the same journey undertaken by her father-in-law Abraham. She chooses to leave her homeland and follows the directive of God. Rebekah, not her husband, receives the message of God that determines the future of her two sons. She ingeniously carries out her plan to assure that Jacob, her favorite son and God's choice, will carry on the line of the promise. Through her resourceful dedication, she becomes the mother of Israel.

Leah and Rachel struggle with God over the foundations of the house of Jacob. The women's fight for God's attention and concern results in the birth of Jacob's twelve sons, who become the tribes of Israel. The women are just as responsible as Jacob for the founding of a nation. However, the story of Dinah, Jacob's only daughter, is a saga of male passion and power, of violence and vengeance, while the desires and feelings of Dinah herself are never disclosed.

Tamar, the daughter-in-law of Judah, could have been another female victim due to the way Judah abandons her to the hopeless state of a childless widow. But Tamar takes matters into her own hands and deceives Judah in order to protect her future. She uses unconventional but imaginative means to integrate herself into Israel's history as an ancestor of the house of Judah. Through the birth of her twins, she makes it possible for the family of Judah to thrive, and Judah declares that she is more honorable than he is.

As the book of Exodus begins, the men are trapped in Pharaoh's bondage, while the women subvert his plans with nonviolent resistance. In an act of solidarity across social and ethnic barriers, the mother and sister of Moses plot with the daughter of Pharaoh to save the one who will rescue the Israelites. Miriam, the sister of Moses, then allies herself with Moses to become one of the leaders of the people in their exodus and wilderness periods.

The Torah demonstrates the interdependence of women and men. In each generation of Israel's patriarchs, there is a parallel matriarchy of mothers, wives, and daughters who play indispensable roles in advancing the identity and destiny of God's people. Though they often work behind the scenes in less public roles, these strong and determined women are as important in the development of Israel as the male heroes.

The Torah presents us with women of flesh and blood, women with tragic faults, powerful passions, and heroic virtues. We'll admire one woman's faith while wondering why another chose the path she pursued. What is most striking is how constant the issues of women have remained from ancient times to the present, for the essence of living has changed very little. The ways God worked in their lives can inform us about the ways God works in our lives. Each woman inspires us, warns us, or leads us. Like us, they fail more often than they succeed. But through their failing, they painfully move forward to solve their problems and confront the challenges of life. Each generation is linked to the next by a shared commitment to lead lives marked by compassion, justice, and love. From the women of the Torah we can learn how to live faithfully in a less than perfect world.

Questions to Consider

‡ How does the truth that men and women are made equally in the image of God affect the ways that women are portrayed in the narratives of Scripture?

✢ What similarities might I find between the lives of the women of the Torah and the lives of women today?

Listen to Sarah, the Quarry of Encouragement

Lectio

Listen to this prophetic voice calling God's people to remember the lives of their ancestors Abraham and Sarah. Pay attention to the way the prophet exhorts people of every age to gain wisdom and strength in the present challenges.

ISAIAH 51:1–2

> ¹Listen to me, you that pursue righteousness,
> you that seek the LORD.
> Look to the rock from which you were hewn,
> and to the quarry from which you were dug.
> ²Look to Abraham your father
> and to Sarah who bore you.

Through this commentary, continue seeking the significance of this passage to help you look to your biblical ancestors, obtaining insights from them into life's purpose and meaning.

This passage from the prophet Isaiah was written during the exile of the Jewish people in Babylon (sixth century BC). Though the exiles have remained faithful to God, they are discouraged and disheartened by their captivity and seeming powerlessness. They fear that, even if they are able to return to Judah, they will not be able to face the overwhelming task of restoring their homeland because they are so weak and few in number. Isaiah offers these exiles an encouraging message, calling them to look back to the example of their ancestors Abraham and Sarah. Though these exiles lived well over a thousand years after Israel's patriarch and matriarch, the prophet still holds up Abraham and Sarah as the inspiring models for their descendants to imitate. In these mentors from the past is found hope for the future.

Based on the parallelism in Hebrew poetry, Abraham is the "rock" from which his descendants were carved and Sarah is the "quarry" from which her descendants were dug. The masculine image of rock suggests an indestructible foundation of solid faith from which later generations were shaped, while the feminine image of quarry implies a rich source from which offspring are mined. Sarah is the deep pit in which are buried valuable minerals and undiscovered treasure. She is the abundant source from which living stones in every generation can be excavated, stones filled with inspiration, courage, faithfulness, and hope.

Based on God's assurances to Abraham and Sarah, the exiles in Babylon can be confident that God will bless them with strength and abundance as they prepare to make the same journey as Abraham and Sarah, returning to their home in the Promised Land. The promises made to Abraham and Sarah continue to be fulfilled in every age. As we reflectively mine the Scriptures for stories of the women of the Torah, we will realize that we are digging in a quarry that will yield plentiful discoveries. Through this work of excavation, we will unearth riches to bring inspiration and hope to our lives.

Meditatio

Consider how these ancient words of the prophet can shine their light into situations of discouragement today.

✢ What might have been some of the discouragement felt by the exiles who listened to the prophet? Do I experience similar discouragement today?

✢ How is studying the stories of the Bible like excavating a quarry? What rich minerals do I hope to mine from this Bible study?

Oratio

Respond to God's Word to you with your own words to God. Speak from your heart in response to the hope you have been offered.

> Most High God, you called our ancestors to a committed life in covenant with you. Help me to learn from their example and be inspired by their heroism so that I may leave a legacy to the generations after me. Bless my life as I listen to, reflect on, and pray through the stories of these women. Transform my life, as you did theirs, with the power of your Word.

Continue to express your hopes, desires, struggles, and commitment . . .

Contemplatio

Remain in peaceful quiet and place yourself in God's loving embrace. Ask God to give you whatever gift he desires for you during these moments.

Operatio

Dedicate yourself to the reflective study of these women of the Torah over the coming weeks. Choose a quiet place and time for your regular lectio divina.

1

Male and Female in the Image of God

Light a candle, ring a chime, or perform some other gesture to sanctify this time and space for encountering God through the words of the inspired Scripture. Read this familiar passage as if for the first time, letting go of all your expectations of what you suppose it will say.

GENESIS 1:26–2:3

²⁶Then God said, "Let us make humankind in our image, according to our likeness; and let them have dominion over the fish of the sea, and over the birds of the air, and over the cattle, and over all the wild animals of the earth, and over every creeping thing that creeps upon the earth."

²⁷So God created humankind in his image,
in the image of God he created them;
male and female he created them.

²⁸God blessed them, and God said to them, "Be fruitful and multiply, and fill the earth and subdue it; and have dominion over the fish of the sea and over the birds of the air and over every living thing that moves upon the earth."

²⁹God said, "See, I have given you every plant yielding seed that is upon the face of all the earth, and every tree with seed in its fruit; you shall have them for food. ³⁰And to every beast of the earth, and to every bird of the air, and to everything that creeps on the earth, everything that has the breath of life, I have given every green plant for food." And it was so.

³¹God saw everything that he had made, and indeed, it was very good. And there was evening and there was morning, the sixth day.

¹Thus the heavens and the earth were finished, and all their multitude. ²And on the seventh day God finished the work that he had done, and he rested on the seventh day from all the work that he had done. ³So God blessed the seventh day and hallowed it, because on it God rested from all the work that he had done in creation.

After reading these verses, continue listening for God's Word in the text as you study this commentary.

This creation account serves as an introduction to the whole Torah, even to the entire Bible. It expresses the inspired reflection of ancient Israel on the nature of God and the world as well as the nature of man and woman in relationship to God. It is written as a poetic and ceremonial hymn, using the seven-day week as a template for describing God's creation. At the climax of creation, as its crowning jewel, God creates humankind.

The word for humankind (*'adam*, in Hebrew) is a collective term representing all people (vv. 26–27). God creates humankind in the divine image and equally as "male and female." God's image in the world is composed of an equal and mutual joining of the marvelous qualities of both male and female. This original identity of the male and the female means that in the essence of being human there is no qualitative difference between being male or female. The male and the female are equally valuable before God. According to the divine plan for creation, male and female share equal privilege and bear equal responsibility within the created world.

The idea of humanity made in the image and likeness of God is perhaps the most glorious and empowering assertion in the Bible. It is the foundation of all Judeo-Christian ethics about human dignity and value as well as teachings about human rights and responsibilities. In addition, it creates within each individual person an irreplaceable personal identity and an impervious self-esteem. Being made in God's image endows us with a spiritual center that we can carry with us throughout all of life's circumstances. If women and men are created in the image of our infinite God, then our potential for spiritual conversion and development is without limit.

In ancient Mesopotamia and Egypt, the regions of the ancient world surrounding Israel, the kings and pharaohs were honored as being made in the image of the gods. This meant that a ruler was the representative of the gods on earth, sharing in the authority and privilege of the divine world. Genesis marks an expansion of this idea to every human being. Every man and woman is a king or queen before his or her Creator, a royal representative of God in the world.

God bestows upon the male and female "dominion" (v. 28) over the fish, birds, animals, and the rest of the visible world. This royal terminology suggests that humankind is given authority over and responsibility for the well-being and enhancement of creation. Human beings must rule the earth as God rules creation. This governance means that women and men must promote the welfare of the other creatures of the earth just as a monarch is charged with the care of a kingdom's citizens. Human beings are accountable to God as his royal representatives and must govern wisely and care for God's kingdom.

Throughout Israel's history and literature, there was a strong prohibition concerning the making of any image of God. This resistance to idolatry was meant to affirm the transcendence of God and humanity's inability to capture or contain God's freedom and power. Israel was forbidden to make any fixed, casted, or molten image of the divine presence. Yet, the Bible's prologue dramatically proclaims the counterassertion that man and woman are made in the image of God. There is only one way in which God is mirrored in the world—the human creature, male and female, acting as God's cocreators, agents, and viceroys in the world.

After reading the Scripture and commentary carefully, write your answer to this question:

✢ What is the difference between "dominion" and "domination" in terms of humanity's rights and responsibilities within the created world?

Meditatio

After reading this creation account with fresh eyes and ears, consider its deeper implications for your understanding of God as well as yourself.

‡ What new understandings have I gained by reading this passage as if for the first time?

‡ What does the fact that God is imaged as male *and* female indicate about God? What does it suggest to me about the responsibilities of women and men in the created world?

‡ What does humanity's royal role in the world indicate about God's command to exercise dominion over the rest of creation?

Oratio

Use the words and images of Scripture in a prayerful and personal response to God's Word.

Wise Creator, you made woman and man in your image and gave us noble privileges and regal responsibilities as your royal representatives in the world. May we rule the earth as you rule creation, always aware of our calling to be accountable agents of your creative energy and love.

Continue to pray to God from your heart . . .

Contemplatio

God looked at all of creation and declared it to be "very good." Spend some time in contemplation, deepening your awareness of the goodness of God's creation, which surrounds you.

After a period of quiet attentiveness, write a few words about your experience.

Operatio

How can I better demonstrate that I take seriously my stewardship of the earth? What can I do today to express my loving responsibility to the world?

2

Woman, the Partner
of Man

Lectio

As you read the Scripture and commentary, highlight or underline passages that seem most pertinent to you. Be sure you do not impose your own preconceived understandings of the author's meaning and intent.

GENESIS 2:4–25

⁴In the day that the LORD God made the earth and the heavens, ⁵when no plant of the field was yet in the earth and no herb of the field had yet sprung up—for the LORD God had not caused it to rain upon the earth, and there was no one to till the ground; ⁶but a stream would rise from the earth, and water the whole face of the ground—⁷then the LORD God formed man from the dust of the ground, and breathed into his nostrils the breath of life; and the man became a living being. ⁸And the LORD God planted a garden in Eden, in the east; and there he put the man whom he had formed. ⁹Out of the ground the LORD God made to grow every tree that is pleasant to the sight and good for food, the tree of life also in the midst of the garden, and the tree of the knowledge of good and evil.

¹⁰A river flows out of Eden to water the garden, and from there it divides and becomes four branches. ¹¹The name of the first is Pishon; it is the one that flows around the whole land of Havilah, where there is

gold; ¹²and the gold of that land is good; bdellium and onyx stone are there. ¹³The name of the second river is Gihon; it is the one that flows around the whole land of Cush. ¹⁴The name of the third river is Tigris, which flows east of Assyria. And the fourth river is the Euphrates.

¹⁵The LORD God took the man and put him in the garden of Eden to till it and keep it. ¹⁶And the LORD God commanded the man, "You may freely eat of every tree of the garden; ¹⁷but of the tree of the knowledge of good and evil you shall not eat, for in the day that you eat of it you shall die."

¹⁸Then the LORD God said, "It is not good that the man should be alone; I will make him a helper as his partner." ¹⁹So out of the ground the LORD God formed every animal of the field and every bird of the air, and brought them to the man to see what he would call them; and whatever the man called every living creature, that was its name. ²⁰The man gave names to all cattle, and to the birds of the air, and to every animal of the field; but for the man there was not found a helper as his partner. ²¹So the LORD God caused a deep sleep to fall upon the man, and he slept; then he took one of his ribs and closed up its place with flesh. ²²And the rib that the LORD God had taken from the man he made into a woman and brought her to the man. ²³Then the man said,

"This at last is bone of my bones
and flesh of my flesh;
this one shall be called Woman,
for out of Man this one was taken."

²⁴Therefore a man leaves his father and his mother and clings to his wife, and they become one flesh. ²⁵And the man and his wife were both naked, and were not ashamed.

Continue searching for the fuller meaning and significance of this passage through the following remarks:

This second narrative unit of the Bible focuses on humankind and the relationships among God, human beings, and the rest of creation. The scene opens on a sterile world, for God has not yet brought rain upon the earth and "there was no one to till the ground" (v. 5); literally, there was no humankind (*'adam*, in Hebrew) to work the ground (*'adama*, in

Hebrew). In this ancient story, the omnipotent Creator of the earth and the heavens is shown to be a loving provider, generously bestowing life and many other gifts upon the human creature.

Like a sculptor, God fashions the human being from the dust of the ground mixed with the moisture that watered the ground. With this wet clay, God shapes the material with his own imprint into the desired form, then God breathes life into his creature (v. 7). This archetypal human being has no gender distinctiveness but is simply called "the man" (*ha'adam*, in Hebrew), literally, "the human." As in the previous description of the creation of humankind in God's image, the human contains both male and female potential, but there is no division into male and female until the woman is formed.

This generous God then plants a delightful garden and gently places his newly created human creature there (v. 8). The garden is full of beautiful and nourishing trees, including the tree of life and the tree of knowledge. The garden is watered by a river that flows out of the garden and divides into four branches. This bountiful God not only offers gifts in abundance but also infuses the garden with his presence and continually offers care and companionship.

In striking contrast to God's frequent description of creation as "good," God declares that it is "not good" for a person to be alone (v. 18). So unable to find a partner for his human creature from the animals of the earth, God fashions a woman from the human's rib. Rather than making her from the dust, God forms her from the bone and flesh of the man's side. This underscores that the woman is made of the same substance as the man and, unlike the animals, on the same level as the man. Only now are the two human creatures distinguished according to gender. The pair is called man (*'ish*, in Hebrew) and woman (*'ishah*). The similarity of these two Hebrew words highlights the fact that the man and the woman may find a true counterpart in each other.

The creation of woman is the crowning event of the story and the fulfillment of humankind. Describing the woman as a "helper" (v. 18) to the man does not imply a subordinate place, especially considering that God is frequently described as Israel's "helper." The text describes, rather, the mutual support and companionship offered by woman and man for each other. The first human words in the Bible are a poem in praise of woman (v. 23). As the same flesh and bone, man and woman are equal in value, though wonderfully diverse in gender. Bonded in companionship and enriched by their sexual differences, they overcome aloneness and experience fulfillment. Their nakedness and lack of shame express their total intimacy and respectful trust.

Meditatio

Reviewing your highlights from the text and commentary, consider the new insights and modern implications of this ancient narrative.

✝ It has been suggested that the competitiveness and resentment often expressed between men and women today is a result of mutual insecurity. How can the Genesis narrative help increase self-confidence in our God-given uniqueness and dignity?

✝ How does this ancient story assert the interdependence of woman and man? In what ways do women and men need each other to overcome our aloneness and realize our fullest human potential?

✝ Finding a soul mate feels like discovering a hitherto lost and unknown part of oneself. How does Genesis describe the man's response to the woman as the discovery of the missing part of one's self?

Oratio

Using the images and feelings generated by this Scripture passage, spend some time praying to God in words that flow from your heart.

Generous Creator, you fashioned man and woman with your own imprint and breathed into them your life-giving Spirit. Help us be grateful for the gifts, freedom, and purpose you have given to us, and help us to rejoice with delight in your presence.

Continue to pray in whatever words arise from within . . .

Contemplatio

Breathe slowly in and out, considering the divine breath God has placed within you. Rest in the knowledge that you have been wonderfully fashioned by God.

After a period of wordless contemplation, write a few words about your experience.

Operatio

How does this ancient story help me understand my purpose? In what way can I express that purpose concretely today?

3

Sin and Its Consequences

Try reading this account aloud as the ancient storytellers did. Listen carefully for any messages and meanings that strike you.

GENESIS 3:1–13

¹Now the serpent was more crafty than any other wild animal that the LORD God had made. He said to the woman, "Did God say, 'You shall not eat from any tree in the garden'?" ²The woman said to the serpent, "We may eat of the fruit of the trees in the garden; ³but God said, 'You shall not eat of the fruit of the tree that is in the middle of the garden, nor shall you touch it, or you shall die.'" ⁴But the serpent said to the woman, "You will not die; ⁵for God knows that when you eat of it your eyes will be opened, and you will be like God, knowing good and evil." ⁶So when the woman saw that the tree was good for food, and that it was a delight to the eyes, and that the tree was to be desired to make one wise, she took of its fruit and ate; and she also gave some to her husband, who was with her, and he ate. ⁷Then the eyes of both were opened, and they knew that they were naked; and they sewed fig leaves together and made loincloths for themselves.

⁸They heard the sound of the LORD God walking in the garden at the time of the evening breeze, and the man and his wife hid themselves from the presence of the LORD God among the trees of the garden. ⁹But the LORD God called to the man, and said to him, "Where are

you?" [10]He said, "I heard the sound of you in the garden, and I was afraid, because I was naked; and I hid myself." [11]He said, "Who told you that you were naked? Have you eaten from the tree of which I commanded you not to eat?" [12]The man said, "The woman whom you gave to be with me, she gave me fruit from the tree, and I ate." [13]Then the LORD God said to the woman, "What is this that you have done?" The woman said, "The serpent tricked me, and I ate."

After carefully reading the inspired text, keep searching for its fullest significance through this commentary.

As the ancient story of the garden continues, the narrator contrasts the blissful innocence of man and woman that God intended and the actual state of humankind in the world. The balanced state of harmony and mutual trust between God and his human creatures in the garden is disrupted through human disobedience. Through human choice, God's purpose for man and woman, with its wide permission and necessary prohibition, is disturbed and distorted.

Into this delightful garden crawls the cunning serpent (v. 1). In a beguiling conversation with the woman, the serpent distorts God's permission and prohibition concerning the fruit of the trees. With enticing seduction the serpent goes on to deny that death would be the inevitable consequence for rejecting the limitations God had placed on them. The tempter suggests instead that the woman and man would be like God, possessing great knowledge and able to determine what is good and what is evil (vv. 2–5). The Lord of the garden, who bestowed such wondrous gifts and abundant freedom, is presented by the serpent as one who wants to confine rather than provide. The safe boundaries God had established for the couple's well-being in the garden now seem to them like a restriction upon their freedom and autonomy.

After considering the serpent's distorted line of reasoning and her newly acquired desire to taste the tree's fruit, the woman "took of its fruit and ate" (v. 6). Then the woman gave some of the fruit to the man with her, "and he ate." The blunt statements point to a deliberate transgression of God's prohibition by both the man and the woman. There is no sense here that the woman enticed the man to disobedience. Though the woman speaks to the serpent, the man "was with her." The serpent uses the plural form when addressing the woman, indicating that the man was near her throughout the conversation. Likewise, the woman uses the plural form in speaking with the serpent, demonstrating that she was speaking for herself as well as for the man. His silence and failure to enter the debate can be interpreted as agreement with the woman. When the fruit is offered, he can certainly refuse, but they act in total accord.

The consequences of the disobedience of man and woman begin to unfold immediately, shattering the harmony and trust between God and humankind as well as between the man and the woman. Rather than opening their eyes to the unlimited knowledge and independence for which they had hoped, they become aware of their own nakedness and shame (v. 7). When God comes to walk in the garden among his creatures, the man and the woman hide themselves in fear (v. 8). When God confronts the man, he blames the woman (v. 12). When God challenges the woman, she blames the serpent (v. 13).

In the garden, God provided man and woman with life, beauty, abundance, freedom, harmonious relationships, meaningful purpose, work, and leisure. The human choice to transgress God's desire brings shame, self-consciousness, guilt, fear, mistrust, self-justification, blame of others, and evasion of responsibility. This ancient story offers profound insight into the human predicament. Through representational figures, symbolic language, and Hebrew wordplays, the narrator speaks to and about all women and men. The desires and responses of the man and the woman, and consequently their dilemma, characterize the experience of all humankind. The transgression depicted is not simply the first sin; it is all human sin; it is my sin. We who listen to this ancient story know that our sin too has cosmic dimensions, that our transgressions influence the relationship of humankind with God, that our failure to heed the boundaries God established affects the trustful relationship God wishes to share with his people. The narrative functions as a mirror in which all readers see their own reflections.

After listening to this ancient story of the human condition, think about this question:

✝ What are the indicators in the text that both man and woman are to blame for transgressing God's prohibition?

Meditatio

Allow the text to interact with your own ideas, struggles, dilemmas, and concerns. Reflect on its significance in your own life and the wisdom it offers to you.

‡ Why does the serpent mix the truth with lies in order to distort the statements of God's will for humanity? What does this indicate about the nature of temptation and deception?

‡ In what way does human transgression of boundaries established by the Creator disrupt our harmony with God, fellow humans, and the rest of creation?

‡ From this narrative, how would I define sin and its consequences?

Oratio

Pray to God in response to the message you have heard in God's Word. You may choose to begin with these or similar words:

Faithful God, in your wisdom you have established the purpose, freedom, and limitations of human life and action. Orient my life according to the calling you have given me, guide me in my struggles to know what is good, and give me the humility to admit my failures.

Continue to pray as your heart directs . . .

Contemplatio

In the garden, God asked the man and woman, "Where are you?" Place yourself in the presence of your all-knowing, all-loving God. Trust that God wishes to be with you and bless you with his presence.

After a period of wordless contemplation, write a few words about your experience.

Operatio

Considering the purpose God has given for my life, what can I do today to further that purpose in order to cooperate with God's creative work in the world?

4

Eve, Mother of
All Who Live

Speaking the words of the narrative aloud, read slowly and mark any words or phrases that seem addressed to you personally or strike you in a new way.

GENESIS 3:14–24

> [14]The LORD God said to the serpent,
> "Because you have done this,
> cursed are you among all animals
> and among all wild creatures;
> upon your belly you shall go,
> and dust you shall eat
> all the days of your life.
> [15]I will put enmity between you and the woman,
> and between your offspring and hers;
> he will strike your head,
> and you will strike his heel."
> [16]To the woman he said,
> "I will greatly increase your pangs in childbearing;

in pain you shall bring forth children,
yet your desire shall be for your husband,
and he shall rule over you."

¹⁷And to the man he said,

"Because you have listened to the voice of your wife,
and have eaten of the tree
about which I commanded you,
'You shall not eat of it,'
cursed is the ground because of you;
in toil you shall eat of it all the days of your life;
¹⁸thorns and thistles it shall bring forth for you;
and you shall eat the plants of the field.
¹⁹By the sweat of your face
you shall eat bread
until you return to the ground,
for out of it you were taken;
you are dust,
and to dust you shall return."

²⁰The man named his wife Eve, because she was the mother of all who live.

²¹And the LORD God made garments of skins for the man and for his wife, and clothed them.

²²Then the LORD God said, "See, the man has become like one of us, knowing good and evil; and now, he might reach out his hand and take also from the tree of life, and eat, and live forever"— ²³therefore the LORD God sent him forth from the garden of Eden, to till the ground from which he was taken. ²⁴He drove out the man; and at the east of the garden of Eden he placed the cherubim, and a sword flaming and turning to guard the way to the tree of life.

After allowing the text to penetrate your mind and heart, continue searching for the significance of these ancient words of Scripture.

The Genesis story shows that the disharmony that men and women experience with God, one another, and the rest of creation came about because of their striving for autonomy apart from God. This disordered world is represented by the continual enmity between the serpent's progeny and the woman's. The twisted and snaky temptations lurking in the underbrush will strike at the heels of the woman's offspring while they try to stave off the enticing assaults (v. 15). Women will bring forth children with great pains, and even though they are attracted to their husbands, they will be dominated by them (v. 16). Men will work the land with wearisome toil and sweaty labor to bring forth food to eat (vv. 17–19). Finally, men and women will die and return to the ground from which they came.

Yet, even in judgment, God's grace is continually evident. Though the sentence seems heavy, it is less than the death that was pledged. God continues to insist on life for his creatures, albeit life at a distance from the garden and apart from the immortality provided by the tree of life. As a consequence of human transgression, this life includes elements of pain, fear, anxiety, alienation, and mistrust. Yet, God remains present with his human creatures, clothing them with garments of skins for their protection and comfort and offering them his attentive care and hope.

These opening chapters of Genesis have been used throughout history to justify the subordination of women. First, it is argued that woman is created derivatively from the primary creature, which is man. Second, it is argued that woman is the temptress of the man, leading him to sin. Third, it is argued that part of woman's destiny is to be ruled by the man. Yet, these points of view cannot be supported by the biblical texts and are good examples of the ways our cultural assumptions influence our interpretations.

A careful reading of the text demonstrates that the subordination of women is contrary to God's creative desires. In the first place, the creation of the woman from the flesh and bone of the human creature is the act that initiates gender distinctiveness. The woman is not formed in imitation of the man; rather, she is fashioned as the culmination of creation. Following the creation of woman, the story of human disobedience is described as a mutual action. Both man and woman heard the enticing words of the serpent, and both chose to eat the fruit of the tree. Finally, the man's rule over the woman is the result of the distorted human condition brought about by sin and not the norm established by the Creator. The will of God for women and men, as represented by the garden, is equality and mutuality. The human predicament in the world, as represented by the eviction from the garden, is dominated by mistrust and control.

Only at the end of the account in the garden is the woman given a name: "The man named his wife Eve, because she was the mother of all who live" (v. 20). The name resembles the Hebrew word for "life" and honors the woman's awesome ability to cultivate new life. Because of God's grace, the inevitable death of man and woman becomes a fruitful mortality, and Eve becomes a sign of life and hope for humankind.

Meditatio

In your reflection, seek to find the meaning of this text for you and the personal message you might gain from your study.

‡ What indicates that male domination is a consequence of sin and not part of the created nature of humanity? In what ways do these accounts stress the essential equality and mutuality between man and woman?

‡ God's gift of clothing for the woman and the man helps them prepare for life outside the garden. What does this tell me about God and his response to my sins?

‡ Who is the offspring of Eve who will finally strike the serpent's head with a fatal blow (Rom. 16:20)? What, then, is the fuller meaning of the ongoing strife between the serpent and the offspring of Eve?

Oratio

Speak to God in response to your lectio and meditatio.

Gracious God, the disorder that sin creates has distorted the goodness and freedom you desire for your creatures. Be with us in our struggles outside the garden, as you lead us to the fullness of life for which you created us.

Continue to pray, using whatever words and phrases of the text most touched your heart . . .

Contemplatio

Know that God gives us what we need to live outside the garden. Ask for the gift of trust, realizing that God is blessing you in quiet stillness and enfolding you with grace.

After a period of trusting silence, write a few words about your experience.

Operatio

Eve is the mother of all who live. What maternal role am I able to play today to nurture and care for people?

5

Eve, Adah, Zillah, and Naamah

This text demonstrates the fractured nature of humankind due to the sinful choices of men and women. Think about the global ramifications of these ancient passages.

GENESIS 4:1–7, 16–26

¹Now the man knew his wife Eve, and she conceived and bore Cain, saying, "I have produced a man with the help of the LORD." ²Next she bore his brother Abel. Now Abel was a keeper of sheep, and Cain a tiller of the ground. ³In the course of time Cain brought to the LORD an offering of the fruit of the ground, ⁴and Abel for his part brought of the firstlings of his flock, their fat portions. And the LORD had regard for Abel and his offering, ⁵but for Cain and his offering he had no regard. So Cain was very angry, and his countenance fell. ⁶The LORD said to Cain, "Why are you angry, and why has your countenance fallen? ⁷If you do well, will you not be accepted? And if you do not do well, sin is lurking at the door; its desire is for you, but you must master it."

¹⁶Then Cain went away from the presence of the LORD, and settled in the land of Nod, east of Eden.

¹⁷Cain knew his wife, and she conceived and bore Enoch; and he built a city, and named it Enoch after his son Enoch. ¹⁸To Enoch was

born Irad; and Irad was the father of Mehujael, and Mehujael the father of Methushael, and Methushael the father of Lamech. [19]Lamech took two wives; the name of the one was Adah, and the name of the other Zillah. [20]Adah bore Jabal; he was the ancestor of those who live in tents and have livestock. [21]His brother's name was Jubal; he was the ancestor of all those who play the lyre and pipe. [22]Zillah bore Tubal-cain, who made all kinds of bronze and iron tools. The sister of Tubal-cain was Naamah.

[23]Lamech said to his wives:
"Adah and Zillah, hear my voice;
you wives of Lamech, listen to what I say:
I have killed a man for wounding me,
a young man for striking me.
[24]If Cain is avenged sevenfold,
truly Lamech seventy-sevenfold."

[25]Adam knew his wife again, and she bore a son and named him Seth, for she said, "God has appointed for me another child instead of Abel, because Cain killed him." [26]To Seth also a son was born, and he named him Enosh. At that time people began to invoke the name of the LORD.

Continue seeking the meaning of these ancient texts through this commentary.

These genealogical stories of the descendants of Adam and Eve are told not so much for their chronological value but as a demonstration of the fractured nature of our world outside the garden. Within human nature is the desire to bring forth new life and create human culture, but, at the same time, there is a tendency toward rage, revenge, and violence. These texts show that human progress in the world includes attempts to worship God, build civilization, develop industry, and create the arts, but the urge to sin is constantly "lurking at the door" (v. 7). The human task is to subdue our destructive impulses and channel them in creative and constructive ways to advance a civilization of love.

Framing these accounts of vengeance and murder is the report of Eve giving birth to her children, a demonstration that God has not abandoned humanity but that God's grace triumphs over human sin (vv. 1, 25). As "the mother of all who live" (3:20) she rejoices in her fertility and proclaims that she has participated with God in the act of creation. Identifying her first offspring as "a man" (4:1) rather than a son or a child indicates a wordplay. She had been taken from "a man" (*'ish*) and thus called "a woman" (*'ishah*); now she, a woman, has produced "a man" (*'ish*). Woman was formed from man; now man is formed from woman.

The family is always fertile ground for the development of jealousy, hurt, anger, and resentment. After giving birth to her first two children, Cain and Abel, Eve realizes that child rearing is a mixed blessing. The tragic tale of these brothers begins in devotion to God and ends in bloodshed. Because Abel presents the choicest portion of his flock in an offering acceptable to God, Cain responds with envious rage (vv. 4–5). Then, falling victim to his own dark impulses, Cain takes his brother into the field and commits murder.

Eve represents all grieving mothers who witness domestic violence, the death of their children, the tragedies of family life. She learns the deeper meaning of God's words, "in pain you shall bring forth children" (3:16). Love and rage are closely linked in family relationships. The sin of jealous violence, emotional abuse, physical cruelty, and even murderous bloodshed is crouching just outside the door of our homes.

Based on the text describing Cain's family, we may assume that Cain later learned to master his destructive impulses and channel his aggression into building a city (v. 17). Though the narrative does not mention who the wife of Cain is, we may presume that he married one of Adam's daughters, since a later note in the text indicates that Adam had "other sons and daughters" (5:4).

Lamech took two wives, as was common in ancient cultures (4:19). Their names were Adah, a name meaning "adornment, decoration," and Zillah, meaning "tinkling cymbal." These two women, along with Zillah's daughter, Naamah, are the only women mentioned in an otherwise all-male genealogy. If the names of Adah and Zillah are taken with Naamah, a name that means "singer," then all the women are associated with aspects of artistic expression. Their inclusion here highlights the essential role of women in the development of civilization. When the male children are added with their unique gifts of shepherding, musical performance, and metalworking, we see the expression of civilized culture arising in the midst of the fragmented world (vv. 20–22).

Meditatio

Think about the deeper implications of this Scripture on your understanding and living the faith.

✝ How does Eve discover that rearing children is even more painful than birthing children? In what ways have I experienced the bittersweet nature of forming a family?

✝ What does the story of Cain and Abel tell me about the spirit in which I must make my offerings to God? What does Jesus say about such offerings (Matt. 5:23–24)?

✝ Statistics indicate that the majority of violent crimes are committed between family members and close acquaintances. What does this say about the links between love and rage?

Oratio

Offer praise to God for the wondrous ways he is revealed to you as the Creator and Sustainer of the world.

Lord God, you continue to be gracious in the midst of human sin, and you desire to save even when we ignore your presence. Continue to guide me along the path of life when the temptation to sin lurks all around me.

Continue to implore God's help through the challenges of this fragmented world.

Contemplatio

Consider your favorite piece of artistic expression. Let the sight, sound, or memory of that creative work lead you to a deep gratitude for the beauty that women and men are able to create even in this imperfect world.

After a period of grateful quiet, write a few words about your experience.

Operatio

The human task is to subdue our destructive impulses and channel them in creative and constructive ways to advance a civilization of love. How can I participate in this task today?

6

Noah's Wife and the Wives of His Sons

Be aware of your breathing as you create a sacred space within you. Prepare to listen to this sacred text by asking the Holy Spirit to guide your understanding.

GENESIS 7:1–16; 8:14–19

¹Then the LORD said to Noah, "Go into the ark, you and all your household, for I have seen that you alone are righteous before me in this generation. ²Take with you seven pairs of all clean animals, the male and its mate; and a pair of the animals that are not clean, the male and its mate; ³and seven pairs of the birds of the air also, male and female, to keep their kind alive on the face of all the earth. ⁴For in seven days I will send rain on the earth for forty days and forty nights; and every living thing that I have made I will blot out from the face of the ground." ⁵And Noah did all that the LORD had commanded him.

⁶Noah was six hundred years old when the flood of waters came on the earth. ⁷And Noah with his sons and his wife and his sons' wives went into the ark to escape the waters of the flood. ⁸Of clean animals, and of animals that are not clean, and of birds, and of everything that creeps on the ground, ⁹two and two, male and female, went into

the ark with Noah, as God had commanded Noah. [10]And after seven days the waters of the flood came on the earth.

[11]In the six hundredth year of Noah's life, in the second month, on the seventeenth day of the month, on that day all the fountains of the great deep burst forth, and the windows of the heavens were opened. [12]The rain fell on the earth forty days and forty nights. [13]On the very same day Noah with his sons, Shem and Ham and Japheth, and Noah's wife and the three wives of his sons entered the ark, [14]they and every wild animal of every kind, and all domestic animals of every kind, and every creeping thing that creeps on the earth, and every bird of every kind—every bird, every winged creature. [15]They went into the ark with Noah, two and two of all flesh in which there was the breath of life. [16]And those that entered, male and female of all flesh, went in as God had commanded him; and the LORD shut him in.

[14]In the second month, on the twenty-seventh day of the month, the earth was dry.

[15]Then God said to Noah, [16]"Go out of the ark, you and your wife, and your sons and your sons' wives with you. [17]Bring out with you every living thing that is with you of all flesh—birds and animals and every creeping thing that creeps on the earth—so that they may abound on the earth, and be fruitful and multiply on the earth." [18]So Noah went out with his sons and his wife and his sons' wives. [19]And every animal, every creeping thing, and every bird, everything that moves on the earth, went out of the ark by families.

After listening to the text, continue searching for its full meaning within God's plan.

The general theme of Genesis 3–11 is the fragmented and broken character of the world as a result of human sin. Creation is not unified, harmonious, and whole, as God willed it to be. Instead it is filled with pockets of chaos; pain and suffering are present even in life's best experiences; envy and hatred warp the human heart; and sin is always lurking at the door.

The account of the ark and the flood is one of the first Bible stories mothers tell their children. Kids are fascinated by the floating menagerie inhabited by every kind of creature. In it is a world without violence—where the lamb really does lie down with the lion, and where every animal has its place and its mate. Children instinctively know that this account from Genesis is about safety and security rather than destruction. Noah's ark is a portable home for the world, delivered from the floodwaters by an all-powerful but loving divine parent.

But the story of Noah, his wife, and his sons and daughters-in-law is a tale for adults too. It begins with the disobedience of man and woman and is followed by the fatal aggression of Cain, expressing the effects of sin in the world. In this account, the tide of violence has risen to global dimensions, and humankind is drowning in it. God sees the wickedness and corruption of humankind and knows that his creation is on a downward spiral. Seeing that his purposes and dreams for his beloved creation have no prospect of fulfillment, "the LORD was sorry that he had made humankind on the earth, and it grieved him to his heart" (6:6). The pain of God's heart is described with a word from the same root that was previously used to describe the woman's pain in childbearing (3:16). This is not an enraged judge but a heartbroken parent.

In the dismal darkness of this sin-soaked world, God finds a ray of light. Noah walks with God and has found favor with God. Seeing Noah, his wife, his three sons, and their wives, God dreams of a new beginning, an alternative possibility for creation. When God describes to Noah his new plan for the world, "Noah did all that the LORD had commanded him" (7:5). Here is God's fully responsive human being, amenable to God's will because he knows that God's commands are promises of life.

The story of the flood, so common in the ancient literature of many cultures, forms the dramatic setting for this description of God's grieving, passionate, and saving will for humankind and the world. God is determined not to allow the corruption of humankind to sway him from his dream of harmony and peace for creation. The small family of eight women and men cooperated with God and cared not only for one another but also for every species of bird, mammal, reptile, and insect. Their attentive regard for all of creation reflects the loving concern of God for the preservation of every creature. Yet, this delightful experience of creaturely harmony on the ark does not last after the flood subsides. Humankind remains essentially corrupt and disordered, but God remains steadily committed to his creation and refuses to abandon it to the chaos of its disobedience.

Genesis 3–11, filled with ancient narratives about the way the world ought to be but is not, forms the prologue for the rest of the Bible. These legendary stories show us why we need promises of salvation and why God chooses to get involved in human history with a desire to bring blessings to all the nations of the earth. The accounts of creation and sin prepare us for the narratives of Israel's patriarchs and matriarchs that fill the remaining pages of the book of Genesis.

Meditatio

After reading again the familiar story of the ark and the flood, think about its implications for the world and your own life today.

‡ In what ways do the stories we tell our children influence their understanding of God? What do I most want to communicate to children about God in the stories I tell them?

‡ In what way does this narrative describe the emotions of God in view of the reality of human sin? How does this insight into God's feelings affect the way I understand the meaning of this account?

‡ In what way is Genesis 3–11 a prologue for the rest of the Bible? What can we expect God to do in the remainder of the salvation story?

Oratio

We can be confident that God cares about our lives and remains committed to our salvation. Lift up a confident prayer to your God.

Passionate Creator, your heart grieves when you see corruption and violence within your creation. Give me the compassionate heart of Noah and his wife to see the individual worth of every creature, and give me your commitment to care for the earth.

Continue to pray from your heart . . .

Contemplatio

Spend some moments looking at the world afresh as Noah and his wife might have looked at the new world after the flood. Try to instill within yourself the passionate love of God for all his creatures.

After a period of contemplative silence, write a few words about your experience.

Operatio

If, like Noah and his wife, I were chosen by God to begin the world anew, what understanding and practices would I want to instill within the world's children? What is preventing me from doing that today?

7

Sarai Offers Hagar
to Bear a Child

Lectio

*Vocalize the words of this text so that you not only read them with your eyes
but also hear them with your ears. Try to sense the tensions and emotions
within the narrative.*

GENESIS 16:1–16

¹Now Sarai, Abram's wife, bore him no children. She had an Egyptian slave-girl whose name was Hagar, ²and Sarai said to Abram, "You see that the LORD has prevented me from bearing children; go in to my slave-girl; it may be that I shall obtain children by her." And Abram listened to the voice of Sarai. ³So, after Abram had lived ten years in the land of Canaan, Sarai, Abram's wife, took Hagar the Egyptian, her slave-girl, and gave her to her husband Abram as a wife. ⁴He went in to Hagar, and she conceived; and when she saw that she had conceived, she looked with contempt on her mistress. ⁵Then Sarai said to Abram, "May the wrong done to me be on you! I gave my slave-girl to your embrace, and when she saw that she had conceived, she looked on me with contempt. May the LORD judge between you and me!" ⁶But Abram said to Sarai, "Your slave-girl is in

your power; do to her as you please." Then Sarai dealt harshly with her, and she ran away from her.

⁷The angel of the LORD found her by a spring of water in the wilderness, the spring on the way to Shur. ⁸And he said, "Hagar, slave-girl of Sarai, where have you come from and where are you going?" She said, "I am running away from my mistress Sarai." ⁹The angel of the LORD said to her, "Return to your mistress, and submit to her." ¹⁰The angel of the LORD also said to her, "I will so greatly multiply your offspring that they cannot be counted for multitude." ¹¹And the angel of the LORD said to her,

"Now you have conceived and shall bear a son;
you shall call him Ishmael,
for the LORD has given heed to your affliction.
¹²He shall be a wild ass of a man,
with his hand against everyone,
and everyone's hand against him;
and he shall live at odds with all his kin."

¹³So she named the LORD who spoke to her, "You are El-roi"; for she said, "Have I really seen God and remained alive after seeing him?" ¹⁴Therefore the well was called Beer-lahai-roi; it lies between Kadesh and Bered.

¹⁵Hagar bore Abram a son; and Abram named his son, whom Hagar bore, Ishmael. ¹⁶Abram was eighty-six years old when Hagar bore him Ishmael.

Continue listening for God's Word as you explore this ancient text through this commentary.

The two women presented here, Sarai and Hagar, are strikingly different from each other. Sarai, the wife of Abram, is a beautiful but aging woman who had traveled with her husband to the land of Canaan at the call of God. Hagar is a foreign slave girl, youthful and fertile, serving the mistress of the household. Unable to bear children herself, Sarai takes the initiative and asks her husband to father a child by her Egyptian servant, Hagar (v. 2). This practice of an infertile wife offering a surrogate to her husband from among their slaves seems to be a socially legitimate practice in the ancient Middle East. By this means, Sarai hopes to give Abraham an heir and build their family, since the child would be regarded as the lawful offspring of the wife and husband.

Neither Sarai nor her husband mentions obtaining the consent of Hagar. At the bottom of the social status, even Hagar's sexuality belongs to her mistress. Yet, when Hagar immediately conceives, she realizes that she is more than a substitute womb. She knows she has something Sarai doesn't have, and this awareness causes her to stop honoring Sarai's status above her own (v. 4). When Sarai realizes she has lost authority in her household, she indicts Abram in an attempt to persuade him to restore her influence over her slave. Abram washes his hands of the matter and withdraws all support from the woman who is bearing his child. In turn, Sarai treats Hagar so harshly that the pregnant slave girl flees into the wilderness (v. 6).

The angel of God finds Hagar at an oasis in the desert and addresses her by name, the first time she has been so addressed, asking her about her past and her future: "Where have you come from and where are you going?" (v. 8). Hagar is able to answer the question about her past, but the angel reveals her future. First, she must return to the oppression of her mistress, a necessary period of trial so that her son can be named and claimed by Abraham. She is to name him Ishmael, a name that means "God hears," for indeed God has heard her cry for help and hears the cries of the outcasts. Then her son will be wild and free, and Hagar will have so many offspring that they won't be able to be counted (v. 10). She will be the mother of a great nation, the Arab people, who will be born from the descendants of Ishmael.

In response to God's liberating Word and incredible divine promises, Hagar gives God a name (v. 13). She is the only person in the Bible to do so. "El-roi" means both "the God I have seen" and "the God who sees me." The mutual "seeing" between God and Hagar points to a wondrous solution to the dilemma of her oppression. Although powerless as a female, slave, and foreigner, God hears her, sees her, calls her by name, and makes her the mother of a proud heritage.

Meditatio

Reflect on the broader context of this account of Hagar and Sarai in terms of God's bigger plan and your own life struggles.

✢ What are some of the emotional dynamics at work in the rivalry between Sarai and Hagar? Which of these feelings have I experienced?

✢ God's messenger told Hagar to return and submit to Sarai, but he also promised her future blessings and countless descendants. Why does God's pattern of interaction with his creation always involve a period of trial and suffering before the promised blessings? Have I noticed this pattern in my own life?

✢ The Israelites are a foreign people whom God will rescue from their oppressive captivity. God promises to bless them and make of them a great nation. In what way is the life of Hagar a preview of the story of Israel?

Oratio

Respond to the voice of God you have heard in Scripture through the words of your prayer.

El-roi, God of vision, you are the God who truly sees me and responds to the cry of suffering people. You know the emotional conflicts that rage within me: generosity, jealousy, anger, frustration, and hope. Help me to trust in your plan for my life and my family.

Continue to pray to God in words that rise from your own heart . . .

Contemplatio

When you reach a point in your prayer at which words no longer seem helpful or necessary, just rest in the confidence that God desires to give you a future filled with blessings and salvation.

After a period of quiet contemplation, write a few words about your experience.

Operatio

What does this text teach me about human emotions and their consequences? How can I channel the emotions that swell within me in a way that gives glory to God and furthers God's reign in the world?

8

God Promises
a Son to Sarah

Lectio

Close off the distractions around you and enter a moment of stillness.
Breathe in and out slowly as you prepare to encounter the inspired Word.

GENESIS 17:15–22

¹⁵God said to Abraham, "As for Sarai your wife, you shall not call her Sarai, but Sarah shall be her name. ¹⁶I will bless her, and moreover I will give you a son by her. I will bless her, and she shall give rise to nations; kings of peoples shall come from her." ¹⁷Then Abraham fell on his face and laughed, and said to himself, "Can a child be born to a man who is a hundred years old? Can Sarah, who is ninety years old, bear a child?" ¹⁸And Abraham said to God, "O that Ishmael might live in your sight!" ¹⁹God said, "No, but your wife Sarah shall bear you a son, and you shall name him Isaac. I will establish my covenant with him as an everlasting covenant for his offspring after him. ²⁰As for Ishmael, I have heard you; I will bless him and make him fruitful and exceedingly numerous; he shall be the father of twelve princes, and I will make him a great nation. ²¹But my covenant I will establish with Isaac, whom Sarah shall bear to you at this season next year." ²²And when he had finished talking with him, God went up from Abraham.

After listening carefully to the voice of God in the text, continue to listen for its full meaning and significance.

The context of this passage shows God making a covenant with Abraham and giving him the mark of male circumcision as the covenantal sign. In addition, God changes his name from Abram to Abraham because he will be the father of a multitude of nations. Then into this account, which is seemingly about male covenant bearers, God brings Abraham's wife, Sarai, to the fore. She is included in the covenant with God just as much as Abraham. God changes her name too, from Sarai to Sarah. In changing her name, God changes her destiny from that of a barren woman to the mother of Israel. The name, which means "princess," expresses God's assurances that she will be the royal ancestor of "kings of peoples" who will come forth from her (v. 16).

Abraham and Sarah have been struggling to understand God's promises to give them land, numerous descendants, and blessings. Despite the certainty of God's pledges to them, the fulfillment of the divine promises, especially the conceiving of a child to inherit the promises, has been met with complications and frustrations. At this stage in their lives, they no longer expect the promise of offspring to be fulfilled in the way God had expressed it to them many decades ago. Abraham's only hope for a descendant is in Ishmael, his son with Hagar, so he says to God, "O that Ishmael might live in your sight!" (v. 18). But God insists that the promises are not given to Abraham alone, to be realized with just any woman. The covenant is given to the couple. The son of the promises, therefore, will be Sarah's firstborn son, not Abraham's firstborn.

The stories of Abraham and Sarah up to this point have been tales of disillusionment. Faith always hopes against the evidence, but at some point it withers in the face of unrelenting circumstances while waiting for God to act. Now that the old age of Abraham and Sarah makes it seem impossible that the promises of an heir will be fulfilled, God gives them a reason to keep on believing for one more year. Referring to Abraham's barren wife, Sarah, God says to Abraham, "I will bless her, and moreover I will give you a son by her" (v. 16).

Abraham's reaction to God's extraordinary promise—that his ninety-year-old wife will have a child—is a mixture of faith and doubt. He "fell on his face" (v. 17) in an attitude of reverence before the God whom he still trusts to fulfill his pledges. At the same time, he "laughed" at the idea that a couple as old as he and Sarah can become parents. Yet, God assures him that Sarah's infertility will end and that she will bear their son "at this season next year" (v. 21).

Sarah will be the mother of the covenant, and Isaac, the child of an extraordinary conception, will be the offspring of the promise. Isaac and his offspring will inherit the covenant and its blessings, enjoying a unique relationship with God through the ages. He will forevermore represent the triumph of God's power over human limitations and doubt. Yet, God will not abandon Ishmael and Hagar. God will bless their descendants too, making Ishmael fruitful and his descendents numerous: "He shall be the father of twelve princes, and I will make him a great nation" (v. 20).

In response to God's covenant making with Abraham, he and all the male members of his household are circumcised, marking them with the sign of the covenant on their bodies. Yet, the emphasis on Sarah's role as mother of the covenant assures us that God's covenant is not the exclusive privilege of men. Though the mark of circumcision creates the awareness that a man's sexuality is central to his spiritual identity, a woman's entire body—as it is involved in the child's development in the womb, birthing, and nursing—expresses her spiritual identity as having the potential to co-create life with God. Men have a much more tenuous connection to the mystery of bringing forth new life. By performing the rite of circumcision when his son is eight days old, every father acknowledged God's role in the conception and birth of his son, renewing his own covenant with God and marking the starting point of his child's spiritual journey. A mother's connection with her child is much more physical and intense in its early life than that of a father. From the womb to the breasts, the mother's nurture of her child is a visible reflection of God's tender care for his people.

As Abraham sanctifies his reproductive organ through circumcision, Sarah reenters her reproductive cycle as her body prepares to cultivate the mystery of human life. After enduring the insecurities of infertility and the marital strife of seeking an heir through a surrogate mother, Sarah and Abraham will be blessed with their own child, who will inherit the promises of God's covenant.

Meditatio

Imagine how you would respond to this revealing encounter with God.

‡ Sarai is the only woman in the Bible to be given a new name to signify her new purpose and status in God's plan. Who else today receives a new name in recognition of a spiritual transformation? Is there any way in which my name reflects my spiritual identity?

‡ What might have been the thoughts and emotions of Sarah and Abraham when told they would have a son? Do you think Abraham laughed out of surprise, skepticism, mockery, or joy?

‡ Why is it unnecessary for women to bear a mark of the covenant with God? What are the outward signs of my relationship with God and my trust in his promises?

Oratio

Express the thoughts and feelings that arise within you after reading this Scripture and address them to God.

God of our ancestors, you work wonders in the lives of your people and are eternally faithful to your covenant. Just as Sarah and Abraham never gave up on your grace, help me to trust in the assurances you have given me for the future.

Continue to pray to God from your heart using whatever words you wish . . .

Contemplatio

Consider the hope that God has planted in you. Spend some time in silence cultivating that hope with confident trust in God.

After a period of quiet contemplation, write a few words about your experience.

Operatio

What sign of the covenant would I like to show to the next generation? How can I outwardly demonstrate my relationship with God to a member of the next generation?

9

The Aged Sarah
Laughs at God's Promise

Lectio

Read the passage carefully, stopping to imagine the scene. Think about the sights, sounds, smells, tastes, and touches described here, as well as the emotions of Sarah and Abraham as they encounter God's revealing presence.

GENESIS 18:1–15

¹The LORD appeared to Abraham by the oaks of Mamre, as he sat at the entrance of his tent in the heat of the day. ²He looked up and saw three men standing near him. When he saw them, he ran from the tent entrance to meet them, and bowed down to the ground. ³He said, "My lord, if I find favor with you, do not pass by your servant. ⁴Let a little water be brought, and wash your feet, and rest yourselves under the tree. ⁵Let me bring a little bread, that you may refresh yourselves, and after that you may pass on—since you have come to your servant." So they said, "Do as you have said." ⁶And Abraham hastened into the tent to Sarah, and said, "Make ready quickly three measures of choice flour, knead it, and make cakes." ⁷Abraham ran to the herd, and took a calf, tender and good, and gave it to the servant, who hastened to prepare it. ⁸Then he took curds and milk and the calf that he had prepared, and set it before them; and he stood by them under the tree while they ate.

⁹They said to him, "Where is your wife Sarah?" And he said, "There, in the tent." ¹⁰Then one said, "I will surely return to you in due season, and your wife Sarah shall have a son." And Sarah was listening at the tent entrance behind him. ¹¹Now Abraham and Sarah were old, advanced in age; it had ceased to be with Sarah after the manner of women. ¹²So Sarah laughed to herself, saying, "After I have grown old, and my husband is old, shall I have pleasure?" ¹³The LORD said to Abraham, "Why did Sarah laugh, and say, 'Shall I indeed bear a child, now that I am old?' ¹⁴Is anything too wonderful for the LORD? At the set time I will return to you, in due season, and Sarah shall have a son." ¹⁵But Sarah denied, saying, "I did not laugh"; for she was afraid. He said, "Oh yes, you did laugh."

After listening to this sacred text with your mind and heart, continue exploring its implications through these comments:

The question of the three messengers, "Where is your wife Sarah?" (v. 9) is the type of question we could ask about most of the women in Scripture. Where are they? In the patriarchal world of the Bible, women are often, like Sarah, behind the scenes. They are just out of sight even though the interactions of the biblical narrative assume their significance and involvement. Here Sarah is busy in the tent but listening carefully to the encounter that is primarily about her. In this masterpiece of narrative art, Abraham seems to be the dominant character on the surface. Yet, he gradually fades into the background as the scene is increasingly shown to be about God and Sarah.

Though the narrator tells the reader that this is a divine visit (v. 1), Abraham does not, at first, think there is anything extraordinary about these three travelers. His tent, set in the shade of the oak trees at Mamre, was a welcome place for wayfarers, hospitality being a revered virtue in the ancient world. Abraham honored his three guests by offering them a place of rest and refreshment in the noonday heat. His openhearted cordiality knew no bounds, demonstrating that he recognizes the presence of God in everyone he meets. Only when the strangers ask about Sarah by name and reveal the extraordinary news of her maternity are there any clues for Abraham that he has been entertaining messengers from God (vv. 9–10).

Assuming that the guests' visit is about men's business, Sarah remains hidden, as would every respectable wife, while her husband entertains his male guests. So when the guests inelegantly inquire about his wife, Abraham curtly responds that she is in the tent. From here on, only one guest speaks and reveals the divine message about Sarah (v. 10). She will have a son within the year. Listening from inside the tent, Sarah is so flabbergasted at the silliness of the message that she laughs to herself (v. 12). Since the guest has not seen her, Sarah assumes that the guest has no idea how old she really is. She can't imagine how she and old Abraham could possibly experience sexual pleasure and conceive a child.

The mystery of the speaker's identity is clarified (v. 13). It is the LORD who not only hears Sarah's laughter but also repeats what she is thinking. To the renewed promise of a son in a year's time, God adds the key question of the passage, which opens Sarah's eyes and elicits her awe before the LORD: "Is anything too wonderful for the LORD?" (v. 14). It is clear now that Sarah's listening at the entrance of the tent was not disrespectful eavesdropping on a conversation between men, but that the account places Sarah there so that she can hear the message that is really intended for her.

Like Abraham in the previous scene (17:17), Sarah laughed because she didn't know how else to respond to a suggestion that seemed so absurd. Yet, when challenged about her laughter by the LORD, Sarah denied laughing because she was embarrassed and afraid (v. 15). When she stops laughing, Sarah's realistic assessment of her age and condition gives way to faith. The name of her son, Isaac ("he laughs"), will continually remind her of the unpredictable, even humorous ways that God keeps his promises. Abraham and Sarah have waited all their lives for the fulfillment of the promise of a son. God's question, "Is anything too wonderful for the LORD," asks if God's power is limited to our own expectations of life, or whether we can dare to believe that God will keep his astounding promises to us. Faith is not a reasonable act that fits into the normal scheme of life, but rather the ability to put our trust in what sometimes seems impossible and even laughable.

Meditatio

Having entered into the experience of this scene, think about its purpose in God's plan and its meaning for your own life.

✝ How does Sarah's role in this scene change from beginning to end? In what ways is she shown to be the primary focus of the visitation throughout?

✝ The Talmud says, "Hospitality to wayfarers is greater than welcoming the Divine Presence." Why are we losing the ancient art of opening our homes in welcome, graciously attending to the needs of guests, and leisurely sharing meals with others?

✝ "Is anything too wonderful for the LORD?" (v. 14). In what way might God be challenging me with this question?

Oratio

Express the thoughts and feelings that arise within you after reading this Scripture and address them to God.

Faithful God, from age to age you demonstrate your trustworthiness and fidelity to your promises. Help me to realize that nothing is impossible for you and that I can dare to believe in your astounding promises to us.

Continue to pray to God from your heart in whatever words you wish . . .

Contemplatio

Spend some quiet moments contemplating the wonderful things God has done in the past and imagining what wonderful things God wants to do in your life in the present and future.

After a period of quiet contemplation, write a few words about your experience.

Operatio

In what sense is God telling me that it's never too late? What will I do in response this week?

10

The Wife and
Daughters of Lot

Lectio

Read this shocking and tragic story of Lot and his family in contrast to the obedient lives of Abraham and Sarah. Notice how dispensable his wife and daughters are in this corrupt culture.

GENESIS 19:1–29

¹The two angels came to Sodom in the evening, and Lot was sitting in the gateway of Sodom. When Lot saw them, he rose to meet them, and bowed down with his face to the ground. ²He said, "Please, my lords, turn aside to your servant's house and spend the night, and wash your feet; then you can rise early and go on your way." They said, "No; we will spend the night in the square." ³But he urged them strongly; so they turned aside to him and entered his house; and he made them a feast, and baked unleavened bread, and they ate. ⁴But before they lay down, the men of the city, the men of Sodom, both young and old, all the people to the last man, surrounded the house; ⁵and they called to Lot, "Where are the men who came to you tonight? Bring them out to us, so that we may know them." ⁶Lot went out of the door to the men, shut the door after him, ⁷and said, "I beg you, my brothers, do not act so wickedly. ⁸Look, I have two daughters who have not known a man; let me bring them out to you, and do to

them as you please; only do nothing to these men, for they have come under the shelter of my roof." [9]But they replied, "Stand back!" And they said, "This fellow came here as an alien, and he would play the judge! Now we will deal worse with you than with them." Then they pressed hard against the man Lot, and came near the door to break it down. [10]But the men inside reached out their hands and brought Lot into the house with them, and shut the door. [11]And they struck with blindness the men who were at the door of the house, both small and great, so that they were unable to find the door.

[12]Then the men said to Lot, "Have you anyone else here? Sons-in-law, sons, daughters, or anyone you have in the city—bring them out of the place. [13]For we are about to destroy this place, because the outcry against its people has become great before the LORD, and the LORD has sent us to destroy it." [14]So Lot went out and said to his sons-in-law, who were to marry his daughters, "Up, get out of this place; for the LORD is about to destroy the city." But he seemed to his sons-in-law to be jesting.

[15]When morning dawned, the angels urged Lot, saying, "Get up, take your wife and your two daughters who are here, or else you will be consumed in the punishment of the city." [16]But he lingered; so the men seized him and his wife and his two daughters by the hand, the LORD being merciful to him, and they brought him out and left him outside the city. [17]When they had brought them outside, they said, "Flee for your life; do not look back or stop anywhere in the Plain; flee to the hills, or else you will be consumed." [18]And Lot said to them, "Oh, no, my lords; [19]your servant has found favor with you, and you have shown me great kindness in saving my life; but I cannot flee to the hills, for fear the disaster will overtake me and I die. [20]Look, that city is near enough to flee to, and it is a little one. Let me escape there—is it not a little one? —and my life will be saved!" [21]He said to him, "Very well, I grant you this favor too, and will not overthrow the city of which you have spoken. [22]Hurry, escape there, for I can do nothing until you arrive there." Therefore the city was called Zoar. [23]The sun had risen on the earth when Lot came to Zoar.

[24]Then the LORD rained on Sodom and Gomorrah sulfur and fire from the LORD out of heaven; [25]and he overthrew those cities, and all the Plain, and all the inhabitants of the cities, and what grew on the

ground. ²⁶But Lot's wife, behind him, looked back, and she became a pillar of salt.

²⁷Abraham went early in the morning to the place where he had stood before the LORD; ²⁸and he looked down toward Sodom and Gomorrah and toward all the land of the Plain and saw the smoke of the land going up like the smoke of a furnace.

²⁹So it was that, when God destroyed the cities of the Plain, God remembered Abraham, and sent Lot out of the midst of the overthrow, when he overthrew the cities in which Lot had settled.

Continue exploring the purpose and lessons of the text through this commentary.

The angels, who had delivered such wonderful news to Abraham and Sarah, come with God's judgment to Sodom, where Lot and his wife and daughters are living. Knowing of the citizens' violent hostility against strangers and their lawlessness, Lot urges the angelic visitors to spend the night at his home rather than in the city square. Yet, after Lot has served dinner to his guests, the men of the city form a violent mob and surround Lot's house. They call Lot to bring the visitors outside so they can violently abuse and rape them.

Begging for the safety of his guests, Lot offers to bring out his two virgin daughters to satisfy the brutal lust of the mob. Lot's blind allegiance to the code of hospitality turns his virtue into a vice. In offering his two daughters to the mob, he loses all moral integrity. As the crowd becomes more aggressive, the angels blind the mob and order Lot's family to leave Sodom.

Sodom, and its neighboring city Gomorrah, are the archetypal evil cities of Genesis and permanent reminders of human wickedness and divine judgment. The sin of the city is social corruption, an arrogant disregard for human rights, and a cynical insensitivity to the sufferings of others (Jer. 23:14; Ezek. 16:49). The episode depicted here, with its mob violence and attempted gang rape, is a graphic confirmation of the city's wickedness, which had drawn down the wrath of God.

Yet, Lot and his family seem to maintain an attraction for the cities of the Plain. When told by the angels to depart, Lot lingers until he is forcefully evacuated. When ordered to escape to the mountains, Lot insists on remaining in one of the smaller cities nearby. When warned to flee and not look back, Lot's wife looks back with longing as the city is consumed with fire and brimstone. Her pillar of salt remained a permanent reminder of the danger of delay and indecision in the face of corrupting wickedness.

Meditatio

As you allow this text to create its impression and impact your imagination, consider the personal message this tragic story is offering you.

✤ What could explain Lot's corrupt judgment and appalling compromise in offering his two daughters to the violent mob? What might have been Lot's wife's reaction to his offer?

✤ This chilling account of mob violence illustrates the way that personal accountability is subsumed within the anonymity of the crowd. What are some ways in which people today commit evil within the lawlessness of a group that they would never do individually?

✤ Lot's wife couldn't resist looking back at the life she was leaving in Sodom. In what way does looking back, regretting decisions made, and refusing to move on keep me stuck? How does looking back prevent me from moving forward into the future?

Oratio

Be aware of the thoughts and feelings that have arisen within you while exploring this dreadful narrative. Reply to God in prayer with words that express your response.

> Just and merciful God, the character of your people is determined by their social behavior and their response under pressure. Give me the courage to preserve my integrity in the midst of the crowd and maintain my accountability under the pressure of the group.

Continue to pray to God with honesty and candor . . .

Contemplatio

Relax in the presence of God, who knows your heart better than you know yourself. Realize that God is transforming you from the inside out without your awareness.

After a period of quiet contemplation, write a few words about your experience.

Operatio

What do I need in order to be more authentic and transparent in my relationships with God and other people? How can I begin working toward that goal today?

11

Lot's Daughters
Manipulate Their Father

Lectio

As you read another terrible account of Lot's family, consider the ways that God's people learn from these ancient stories of their ancestors.

GENESIS 19:30–38

³⁰Now Lot went up out of Zoar and settled in the hills with his two daughters, for he was afraid to stay in Zoar; so he lived in a cave with his two daughters. ³¹And the firstborn said to the younger, "Our father is old, and there is not a man on earth to come in to us after the manner of all the world. ³²Come, let us make our father drink wine, and we will lie with him, so that we may preserve offspring through our father." ³³So they made their father drink wine that night; and the firstborn went in, and lay with her father; he did not know when she lay down or when she rose. ³⁴On the next day, the firstborn said to the younger, "Look, I lay last night with my father; let us make him drink wine tonight also; then you go in and lie with him, so that we may preserve offspring through our father." ³⁵So they made their father drink wine that night also; and the younger rose, and lay with him; and he did not know when she lay down or when she rose. ³⁶Thus both the daughters of Lot became pregnant by their father.

[37]The firstborn bore a son, and named him Moab; he is the ancestor of the Moabites to this day. [38]The younger also bore a son and named him Ben-ammi; he is the ancestor of the Ammonites to this day.

Continue searching for the meaning and significance of this narrative by reading these remarks.

The previous scene in Sodom highlighted the distorted judgment that can arise through a mob mentality. Under the pressure of the crowd, Lot offered his daughters to the lust of the rabble. In contrast, this scene shows the depraved reason that results from unwarranted isolation. Cut off from all others, Lot's daughters commit incest with their father in their desperation to bear offspring. In both scenes, Lot and his family had refused to join the family of Abraham in the hills of Canaan. Attracted by the pleasures of urban life, Lot had moved to the cities of the Plain. When those cities were destroyed, he and his two daughters fled to the hills to the east of the Dead Sea rather than join Abraham in the hills to the west. In moving to the cities and then to the east, Lot chose to leave the ideals exemplified by the life of Abraham, forming a contrast in the narrative between the compromised values of Lot and the obedient faith of Israel's patriarch.

Following the traumatic loss of his wife and home, Lot goes with his daughters to live in a cave in the mountains of what would later be called Moab. Living as refugees, far from relatives and cultural norms, the daughters are distressed by their inability to produce children in their prime childbearing years. In their desperation, they devise a scheme to generate offspring through their father. His previous willingness to compromise the honor of his daughters to protect strangers had shown them how family members can be used for selfish and desperate ends.

Though incest was a strong cultural taboo in ancient Israel, the story does not impute bad motives to Lot's daughters. The text makes clear that the two women believed the devastation to be universal, and their isolation convinced them that "there is not a man on earth" to give them children (v. 31). Their motive was the noble goal of continuing the lineage of Lot. Likewise, the story does not directly incriminate Lot. Unlike most cases of father-daughter incest in which the father abuses his position of power and initiates the sexual encounter, Lot did not participate in the action. The text states that each of his daughters got Lot so drunk with wine that "he did not know when she lay down or when she rose" (vv. 33–35). He begot sons through his daughters while unconscious, remaining completely free from guilt.

While the story of Lot and his daughters steers clear of condemning their actions, neither does it glorify their deeds. The situation is one of moral compromise brought on by the poor choices of Lot, which led to his family's sad state of affairs. When Lot offered his daughters to the frenzied mob in Sodom, he relinquished his moral authority as a father. In the isolation of the cave, his daughters were finally in control of their father. While Lot was drunk with wine, they were able to humiliate him and avenge his betrayal.

The story also illustrates Israel's ambiguous relationship with the offspring of Lot and his daughters. The Moabites and the Ammonites were notorious enemies of Israel throughout their history. The drunkenness, manipulation, and incest of their origin ridicule Israel's adversaries. Yet, Israel continued to look upon the people of Moab and Ammon as neighbors and kin. A later descendant of this unnamed mother of Moab, Ruth the Moabite, is also faced with the dilemma of conceiving children when she has no husband. Ruth's assertive and unconventional means led her to become one of Israel's most admired heroes and the ancestor of Israel's greatest king.

Respond to these questions based on your lectio of the Scripture and commentary:

✢ What does the isolated setting of this story add to its understanding?

✢ In what ways does this account illustrate Israel's ambiguous relationship with the Moabites and the Ammonites?

Meditatio

Take some time to ponder the personal implications of this narrative. Reflect on these questions in that spirit of meditation.

‡ In what ways do both the pressure of a crowd and social isolation lower inhibitions and lead people to make excuses for poor choices? How have I experienced these settings as influences on my choices and behaviors?

‡ Reflect on the thoughts and emotions of Lot's daughters in this scene. What might have been some of the cacophony of responses within the minds and hearts of these women?

‡ When I compare Lot, his wife, and his daughters with the family of Abraham, what differences stand out most clearly? What do these differences tell me about the value of obedient faith?

Oratio

Speak to God in response to the words, ideas, and images of your reflective reading.

> Faithful God, you gather a people in your name to live loyally in your covenant. With personal responsibility and communal accountability, you call your people to the experience of obedient faith. Help me to deepen my commitment to live in your promises.

Continue to pray in union with God's people in whatever words you wish . . .

Contemplatio

In silent stillness, receptively allow God to fill your heart with his divine presence. Realize that God is gently guiding you without your conscious awareness. Trust in him.

After this period of contemplation, write a few words about your experience.

Operatio

God calls his people to a balance between personal solitude and communal life with others. What can I do to create a better equilibrium between these two dimensions of discipleship?

12

Sarah Gives Birth and Sends Hagar Away

Lectio

Read this passage aloud so that you will experience the Scripture more fully by seeing it with your eyes, hearing it with your ears, and speaking it with your lips.

GENESIS 21:1–21

¹The LORD dealt with Sarah as he had said, and the LORD did for Sarah as he had promised. ²Sarah conceived and bore Abraham a son in his old age, at the time of which God had spoken to him. ³Abraham gave the name Isaac to his son whom Sarah bore him. ⁴And Abraham circumcised his son Isaac when he was eight days old, as God had commanded him. ⁵Abraham was a hundred years old when his son Isaac was born to him. ⁶Now Sarah said, "God has brought laughter for me; everyone who hears will laugh with me." ⁷And she said, "Who would ever have said to Abraham that Sarah would nurse children? Yet I have borne him a son in his old age."

⁸The child grew, and was weaned; and Abraham made a great feast on the day that Isaac was weaned. ⁹But Sarah saw the son of Hagar the Egyptian, whom she had borne to Abraham, playing with her son

Isaac. [10]So she said to Abraham, "Cast out this slave woman with her son; for the son of this slave woman shall not inherit along with my son Isaac." [11]The matter was very distressing to Abraham on account of his son. [12]But God said to Abraham, "Do not be distressed because of the boy and because of your slave woman; whatever Sarah says to you, do as she tells you, for it is through Isaac that offspring shall be named for you. [13]As for the son of the slave woman, I will make a nation of him also, because he is your offspring." [14]So Abraham rose early in the morning, and took bread and a skin of water, and gave it to Hagar, putting it on her shoulder, along with the child, and sent her away. And she departed, and wandered about in the wilderness of Beer-sheba.

[15]When the water in the skin was gone, she cast the child under one of the bushes. [16]Then she went and sat down opposite him a good way off, about the distance of a bowshot; for she said, "Do not let me look on the death of the child." And as she sat opposite him, she lifted up her voice and wept. [17]And God heard the voice of the boy; and the angel of God called to Hagar from heaven, and said to her, "What troubles you, Hagar? Do not be afraid; for God has heard the voice of the boy where he is. [18]Come, lift up the boy and hold him fast with your hand, for I will make a great nation of him." [19]Then God opened her eyes and she saw a well of water. She went, and filled the skin with water, and gave the boy a drink.

[20]God was with the boy, and he grew up; he lived in the wilderness, and became an expert with the bow. [21]He lived in the wilderness of Paran; and his mother got a wife for him from the land of Egypt.

Continue listening for the fuller purpose of this Scripture in God's saving plan.

In contrast to the sad tales and compromised values of Lot's wife and daughters, the story of Sarah culminates in joyful fulfillment. The text demonstrates that, in God's own time, "the LORD did for Sarah as he had promised" (v. 1). She bore a son named Isaac—a name derived from "laughter"—and her grateful response indicates her joyful sense of humor: "God has brought laughter for me; everyone who hears will laugh with me" (v. 6). God had overcome her grim sterility, and laughter seems the appropriate response to this renewed life and astonishing gift.

A few years later, at the feast celebrating the child's weaning from the breast and the next stage of childhood, Sarah demands that Abraham banish "this slave woman with her son" (v. 10). She knows that Ishmael holds the inheritance rights as Abraham's firstborn son but that if Abraham grants their freedom, Hagar and Ishmael will forfeit their share of inherited property. Though Abraham is in great distress over his emotional conflict between fatherly love for his firstborn and loyalty to his beloved wife, God prompts him to agree to Sarah's demand (vv. 11–12). With the assurance that God will give Ishmael a great future, Abraham reluctantly packs food and a skin of water for Hagar and sends her away with Ishmael the next day (vv. 13–14).

As Hagar and Ishmael wander in the wilderness, the water is soon consumed and Hagar becomes desperate. She sets her child a distance away under a shrub for shade because she cannot bear to watch him die. As she sits anguished in the desert, "she lifted up her voice and wept" (v. 16). God hears her cry and sends a word of hope through the voice of a divine messenger: "Do not be afraid" (v. 17). The angel instructs her to lift the boy up because God is going to make him into a great nation. God then opens the eyes of Hagar, and she sees a well of water from which they drink and fill their skin (v. 19).

After Hager finds a wife for her son in her native Egypt, we know that she becomes the mother of a great nation, the Ishmaelites, or in modern terms, the Arab people. Her story is that of an oppressed woman who serves a more privileged woman. Yet, when she is cast into the desert and cries out to God, her voice is heard and God calms her fears with the promise of a magnificent future. Her story foreshadows the story of Israel: oppressed in slavery, wandering in the desert, crying out to God, guided into a promised destiny. She reminds the Israelites that the fate of the peoples around them is not so different from their own. Hagar and Ishmael are Israel's alter ego, reminding the Israelites that their separateness from other peoples must not cause their denigration of other peoples. As the opposite half of Israel's personality, Hagar and Ishmael call to their minds throughout centuries of history that the politically oppressed and the wandering refugees around them are their other self.

Meditatio

Reflect on the experiences of Sarah and Hagar in light of the ways that God has worked within your own life.

‡ How does this narrative demonstrate the fierce maternal instincts of Sarah and Hagar? How do the two sons benefit from their mothers' single-minded devotion?

‡ Just as a mother cannot forget any of her children, God remembers Hagar within the story of Sarah and her family. Why did the author choose to include the story of Hagar within the patriarchal narratives of Israel's founding literature? In what way is Hagar an essential part of the founding narrative of Israel?

‡ After her expulsion from Abraham's household, Hagar became a single mother, a political refugee, a hungry exile. Who are the people in Hagar's situation today? What does this narrative teach me about marginalized people in light of God's redeeming will?

Oratio

Speak to God in response to the words, ideas, and images of your reflective reading.

God of our ancestors, the gift of a son brought joyful laughter to Sarah, but Hagar's expulsion from the family brought her tearful anguish. As you gave both women a future to hope for, give me the assurance of your promises during times of joy and sorrow.

Use your own words to continue your prayer . . .

Contemplatio

Rest in these comforting words of Isaiah: "Can a woman forget her nursing child, or show no compassion for the child of her womb? Even these may forget, yet I will not forget you." Spend some moments in trusting silence, knowing that our nurturing God will never forget you.

After a period of quiet contemplation, write a few words about your experience.

Operatio

How do the outcasts of our human family remind us of God's care for all? What can I do to demonstrate God's unforgettable love for single mothers, political refugees, and hungry exiles?

13

Rebekah Shows
Her Willing Heart

Lectio

This scene demonstrates the worthy character of Rebekah as Abraham's servant seeks a wife for Isaac. Listen to the narrative with your imagination and with the ear of your heart.

GENESIS 24:10–33

[10]Then the servant took ten of his master's camels and departed, taking all kinds of choice gifts from his master; and he set out and went to Aram-naharaim, to the city of Nahor. [11]He made the camels kneel down outside the city by the well of water; it was toward evening, the time when women go out to draw water. [12]And he said, "O LORD, God of my master Abraham, please grant me success today and show steadfast love to my master Abraham. [13]I am standing here by the spring of water, and the daughters of the townspeople are coming out to draw water. [14]Let the girl to whom I shall say, 'Please offer your jar that I may drink,' and who shall say, 'Drink, and I will water your camels' —let her be the one whom you have appointed for your servant Isaac. By this I shall know that you have shown steadfast love to my master."

[15]Before he had finished speaking, there was Rebekah, who was born to Bethuel son of Milcah, the wife of Nahor, Abraham's brother, coming out with her water jar on her shoulder. [16]The girl was very

fair to look upon, a virgin, whom no man had known. She went down to the spring, filled her jar, and came up. [17]Then the servant ran to meet her and said, "Please let me sip a little water from your jar." [18]"Drink, my lord," she said, and quickly lowered her jar upon her hand and gave him a drink. [19]When she had finished giving him a drink, she said, "I will draw for your camels also, until they have finished drinking." [20]So she quickly emptied her jar into the trough and ran again to the well to draw, and she drew for all his camels. [21]The man gazed at her in silence to learn whether or not the LORD had made his journey successful.

[22]When the camels had finished drinking, the man took a gold nose-ring weighing a half shekel, and two bracelets for her arms weighing ten gold shekels, [23]and said, "Tell me whose daughter you are. Is there room in your father's house for us to spend the night?" [24]She said to him, "I am the daughter of Bethuel son of Milcah, whom she bore to Nahor." [25]She added, "We have plenty of straw and fodder and a place to spend the night." [26]The man bowed his head and worshiped the LORD [27]and said, "Blessed be the LORD, the God of my master Abraham, who has not forsaken his steadfast love and his faithfulness toward my master. As for me, the LORD has led me on the way to the house of my master's kin."

[28]Then the girl ran and told her mother's household about these things. [29]Rebekah had a brother whose name was Laban; and Laban ran out to the man, to the spring. [30]As soon as he had seen the nose-ring, and the bracelets on his sister's arms, and when he heard the words of his sister Rebekah, "Thus the man spoke to me," he went to the man; and there he was, standing by the camels at the spring. [31]He said, "Come in, O blessed of the LORD. Why do you stand outside when I have prepared the house and a place for the camels?" [32]So the man came into the house; and Laban unloaded the camels, and gave him straw and fodder for the camels, and water to wash his feet and the feet of the men who were with him. [33]Then food was set before him to eat; but he said, "I will not eat until I have told my errand." He said, "Speak on."

Continue thinking about the significance of this text as you read the commentary.

After the death of Sarah and before his own death, Abraham knows that he must find a wife for Isaac so that God's promises may be passed on to the next generation. He is resolved to find for Isaac a wife from his old home in Mesopotamia and from among his own kin. Not wanting to send Isaac for fear he would be detained forever by the enticements of city life and knowing himself too old to travel, Abraham sends his most trusted servant to his homeland. He is certain God will lead him to the woman whose heart God has prepared to come to Canaan and become his son's wife. So the servant loads up ten camels with gifts and supplies and sets out for the town where Abraham's brother Nahor lives.

When Abraham's servant arrives, he stops outside of town at the well, a place for social gathering and, in the Bible, a place where men and women meet and where betrothals are often arranged. Since it is evening, the time when the daughters of the townspeople come to draw water, the servant entrusts his mission to God and prays earnestly that God will direct him to the one chosen for Isaac. Before he completes his prayer, "there was Rebekah" coming from the town with the water jar on her shoulder (v. 15).

When the servant asks Rebekah for a sip of water, she not only gives him a drink from her jar but also offers to water his camels, which are thirsty from the journey. Displaying such generosity, strength, and readiness to help, she meets the criteria he has set. He then offers her gold jewelry, demonstrating his conviction that this one is indeed the one God has appointed for Isaac. When the servant discovers that she is from the kindred of Abraham, the characteristic his master had sought for his son's wife, he bows his head and issues a grateful prayer to God.

The servant's prayer of petition (vv. 12–14) and his prayer of praise (vv. 26–27) envelop the scene at the well. His prayer has been answered in a way far more providential than he had imagined. The key term in the prayer is "steadfast love" (hesed, in Hebrew), repeated twice in the petition and again in his prayer of gratitude. This is the word for God's covenanted love in the Bible, and marriage is Israel's favorite image for expressing this love between God and his people. As Isaac was a sign of God's covenant with Abraham and Sarah, so the love between Isaac and Rebekah will express God's steadfast and faithful love.

Meditatio

Reflect on how the inspired text speaks God's Word today in the circumstances of your own life.

‡ Have I ever prayed in a way similar to the servant, asking God for a sign? How appropriate and reliable is this way of discerning God's will?

‡ What does the servant's test of Rebekah at the well tell him about her character? In what way is a willing heart an admirable quality in a husband or a wife?

‡ What are some of the most important considerations for choosing a mate? How would I advise people considering marriage to create a good psychological, emotional, sexual, social, and economic partnership?

Oratio

Respond in prayer to the divine voice you have heard in the sacred text.
Speak to God, like Abraham's servant, in petition and thanksgiving.

O Lord, God of Abraham and Sarah, continue to show me your steadfast love as you guide my decisions as I seek your will. I am grateful for my covenant relationship with you and your faithful care in showing me your way.

Continue to pray to God as your heart directs . . .

Contemplatio

One of the signs of making good decisions is the experience of emotional consolation. Remain in wordless silence, aware of God's presence, enjoying the feeling of comfort that God offers you.

Write a few words about your experience of God in silence.

Operatio

Rebekah went above and beyond duty in not only giving a drink to Abraham's servant but also watering all his camels. How can I go the extra mile today and offer kindness to someone I care about?

14

Rebekah Becomes
the Wife of Isaac

Lectio

*In a comfortable and quiet place, read the Scripture carefully, asking God's
Spirit to guide you in your understanding.*

GENESIS 24:50–67

⁵⁰Then Laban and Bethuel answered, "The thing comes from the
LORD; we cannot speak to you anything bad or good. ⁵¹Look, Rebekah is before you, take her and go, and let her be the wife of your
master's son, as the LORD has spoken."

⁵²When Abraham's servant heard their words, he bowed himself to
the ground before the LORD. ⁵³And the servant brought out jewelry
of silver and of gold, and garments, and gave them to Rebekah; he
also gave to her brother and to her mother costly ornaments. ⁵⁴Then
he and the men who were with him ate and drank, and they spent
the night there. When they rose in the morning, he said, "Send me
back to my master." ⁵⁵Her brother and her mother said, "Let the
girl remain with us a while, at least ten days; after that she may
go." ⁵⁶But he said to them, "Do not delay me, since the LORD has
made my journey successful; let me go that I may go to my master."
⁵⁷They said, "We will call the girl, and ask her." ⁵⁸And they called

Rebekah, and said to her, "Will you go with this man?" She said, "I will." ⁵⁹So they sent away their sister Rebekah and her nurse along with Abraham's servant and his men. ⁶⁰And they blessed Rebekah and said to her,

"May you, our sister, become
thousands of myriads;
may your offspring gain possession
of the gates of their foes."

⁶¹Then Rebekah and her maids rose up, mounted the camels, and followed the man; thus the servant took Rebekah, and went his way.

⁶²Now Isaac had come from Beer-lahai-roi, and was settled in the Negeb. ⁶³Isaac went out in the evening to walk in the field; and looking up, he saw camels coming. ⁶⁴And Rebekah looked up, and when she saw Isaac, she slipped quickly from the camel, ⁶⁵and said to the servant, "Who is the man over there, walking in the field to meet us?" The servant said, "It is my master." So she took her veil and covered herself. ⁶⁶And the servant told Isaac all the things that he had done. ⁶⁷Then Isaac brought her into his mother Sarah's tent. He took Rebekah, and she became his wife; and he loved her. So Isaac was comforted after his mother's death.

Continue listening for the meaning of this story of Rebekah through the commentary.

Rebekah's brother and father give their consent to the marriage, acknowledging that the choice of Rebekah as Isaac's wife "comes from the LORD" (v. 50). The servant then gives thanks to God and bestows costly gifts on Rebekah and her family. After spending the night there, Abraham's servant rises and asks to be sent back to his master with Rebekah. When Rebekah's family hesitates, asking that she remain with them at least ten days, the servant insists that they not be detained since God has brought success to the journey. They decide to settle the matter by letting Rebekah decide. Assuming that she will want to delay, they ask her, and she agrees to leave at once. Echoing the response of Abraham when he was called by God to leave his homeland, Rebekah begins the long journey from Mesopotamia to Canaan in the footsteps of Abraham and Sarah.

The character traits exhibited by Rebekah in these scenes from her youth will stand her in good stead throughout the years of her married life. In her spontaneous response to Abraham's servant who asked for a drink at the well, she shows vigor and generous vitality. When he inquires about her identity, she is articulate and demonstrates self-confidence. She shows warmth and hospitality in inviting the servant to stay with her family. The decisiveness she displays in her decision to leave her homeland exhibits the same responsive, adventuresome spirit shown by her relatives Abraham and Sarah many years before. Like them, she is prepared to leave her comfortable life for the rigors of life in distant Canaan.

The final scene of this charming matchmaking story is the meeting of Isaac and Rebekah when she arrives in Canaan. The couple spot each other from afar. When Rebekah discovers that the man walking toward them is Isaac, she covers her face with her veil (v. 65). Isaac brings Rebekah into the tent of his mother, Sarah, and takes her as his wife. His love for her brings him comfort after his mother's death. The bridge between generations is now complete.

Marriage benefits not only the husband and the wife but also the past and future generations: grandparents and parents, as well as children and grandchildren. The generations provide structure, stability, and nurture for one another. Rebekah and Isaac look back to their parents and grandparents for the roots of their identity and for inspiration. They look forward to the children they will bear and the grandchildren they will share. Anticipation of these future generations gives them hope and expectation. The generations of our families form our personal histories, our sense of belonging, and our lasting continuity.

This entire matchmaking story is a profound statement of God's faithfulness. Though God is not directly active in the narrative, all the events are under God's providential care. No part of Rebekah's call to Canaan lies beyond the purpose of God. This worldview of faith, held by the people of ancient Israel and the writers of this literature, shows us that we can reflect on the experiences of our lives in retrospect and see the amazing movement of God. Events that occur seemingly randomly in the present can be given meaning and credited to God through subsequent reflection and discernment. This view of life ties together the generations so that personal history becomes sacred history.

Meditatio

After reflecting on this passage, ask yourself how the text expands your understanding of God's guidance in your own life.

✝ What are the character traits of Rebekah that stand out most to me? In what way will these traits help make her a good spouse and mother?

✝ In what ways does the marriage of Isaac and Rebekah serve both past and future generations? How do grandparents, parents, children, and grandchildren establish the continuity of my life story?

✝ In what ways am I able to reflect on the events of my life and in retrospect see the amazing guidance of God?

Oratio

Pray to God, who is faithful to his people in the past, present, and future.

God of steadfast love, the marriage of Isaac and Rebecca expresses your faithfulness to the covenant in every generation. Help me to trust my future to you, knowing that you will guide my path in the way you have marked out for me.

Continue praying to God in words that arise from within the fear and confidence of your heart . . .

Contemplatio

God holds all the events of your life—past, present, and future—under his providential care. Spend some moments in trusting silence, knowing that God embraces you with steadfast love.

Write a few words describing your contemplative experience of God's care.

Operatio

What could I do to bind myself more closely with the younger or older generations of my family?

15

Rebekah Gives Birth
to Two Nations

Lectio

Close off the distractions of the day and enter a still moment. Read this text aloud so that you hear the words and listen to the inspired message.

GENESIS 25:19–28

¹⁹These are the descendants of Isaac, Abraham's son: Abraham was the father of Isaac, ²⁰and Isaac was forty years old when he married Rebekah, daughter of Bethuel the Aramean of Paddan-aram, sister of Laban the Aramean. ²¹Isaac prayed to the LORD for his wife, because she was barren; and the LORD granted his prayer, and his wife Rebekah conceived. ²²The children struggled together within her; and she said, "If it is to be this way, why do I live?" So she went to inquire of the LORD. ²³And the Lord said to her,

"Two nations are in your womb,
and two peoples born of you shall be divided;
the one shall be stronger than the other,
the elder shall serve the younger."

²⁴When her time to give birth was at hand, there were twins in her womb. ²⁵The first came out red, all his body like a hairy mantle; so they named him Esau. ²⁶Afterward his brother came out, with his

hand gripping Esau's heel; so he was named Jacob. Isaac was sixty years old when she bore them.

27When the boys grew up, Esau was a skillful hunter, a man of the field, while Jacob was a quiet man, living in tents. 28Isaac loved Esau, because he was fond of game; but Rebekah loved Jacob.

After listening to this Scripture, continue seeking its fuller meaning through this commentary on Israel's ongoing experience of God.

Like Sarah, Rebekah is unable to have children. Barrenness again marks the human terrain from which the fulfillment of God's promises arises. There are no guarantees in life. Family claims, rights, and certitude concerning the future are deceptive. Only prayer ends Rebekah's infertility. Isaac and Rebekah must trust in the power of God (v. 21).

But when Rebekah finally does conceive, she experiences pregnancy as more of a burden than a blessing. Her twins, Jacob and Esau, struggle with one another inside her womb. In that watery darkness, the two bodies kick and wrestle, fighting for nourishment and for a space apart from the other. Racked by pain, Rebekah becomes so miserable that she cries out to God, "Why do I live?" (v. 22).

God's response to Rebekah, in the form of a prenatal oracle, overshadows the coming narrative and offers a preview of her future family (v. 23). Already the lives of Rebekah's children are decisively shaped by the God who spoke them into life. The revelation speaks of the destiny of Jacob and Esau, a future that is not explained but can only be accepted as part of the purpose of God. The oracle is about divine inversion of the way the world is humanly organized. The conventional order insists that the older son should have primacy, with all of its rights and privileges. God's inverting promise, "The elder shall serve the younger," claims that Esau's birth order does not necessarily give him preeminence. Jacob is a scandal even from the beginning, a man of conflict who embodies the alignment of God's promises with the "younger," which, in the ancient world, is the one without power or rights.

As Rebekah's labor begins, the two infants jockey for position in the birth canal. Esau, the stronger, fights his way into the light, winning the status of firstborn son. Then Jacob emerges, "with his hand gripping Esau's heel," seemingly to pull his brother back inside (v. 26). Because Esau wins the first round of their sibling rivalry, Jacob will forevermore be playing catch-up.

At birth, Esau is ruddy and already covered with hair. His reddish complexion points to the name of the land that his descendants will inhabit, Edom, which means "red." His bushy body corresponds to Seir, which means "hairy," the area where Esau will settle. The second twin is named Jacob, "one who grasps the heel," for he will be a finagler, a trickster. He will not be content to be the lesser. As they grow into manhood, Esau loves the outdoors and becomes a skillful hunter. His father, Isaac, naturally sees his robust firstborn as the spiritual heir of the promises God has given his family. In contrast, Jacob is quiet, preferring to live in tents. Like his descendants, the people of Israel, Jacob is a shepherd. Rebekah prefers Jacob, and her love for him will be the critical influence in the way the oracle is fulfilled, the way her younger son will achieve his destiny as the preeminent heir.

After you have listened for the Word of the Lord, answer these questions:

✝ What is the role of prayer in this account?

✝ How does the story of Jacob's birth prefigure his personality?

✝ In what sense does Rebekah give birth to two nations?

Meditatio

Reflect on this birth narrative of Rebekah and her children. Consider the ways that it establishes the pattern of God's action in human life.

‡ What is the significance of maternal infertility in the narratives of Israel's history? How does barrenness in Rebekah's life influence the way she responds to God?

‡ The divine oracle given to Rebekah seems to anticipate the gospel pronouncement that "many who are first will be last, and the last will be first" (Matt. 19:30). In what ways is this pattern displayed in the stories of the Bible?

‡ The "younger," the one in the ancient world without power or rights, includes the widow, the orphan, the sojourner, the refugee. In what ways do I experience God inverting the established order of the world?

Oratio

Pray to God like Rebekah and Isaac did, confident that God will hear you and grant what you need.

> God of our ancestors, through Rebekah, the chosen mother of Israel, you revealed your favor for the powerless and the outcast. Help me to realize that you overturn the ways of power and privilege in the world to establish the ways of your kingdom. Look with favor on my lowliness and lift me up in your sight.

Continue voicing the prayer that issues from your heart . . .

Contemplatio

God is always present in the world with subversive grace, overturning your conventional ways of thinking and establishing his divine inversion. Be silent before this dangerous God and open your life to the power of his grace.

Write a few words about your time of contemplatio.

Operatio

How is God overturning my established way of thinking and converting my heart to the new order of his reign?

16

Rebekah Wins the Blessing for Jacob

Lectio

Listen to this narrative of Rebekah's scheme to secure the patriarchal blessing for Jacob. See if you can come to a new understanding of this well-known text.

GENESIS 27:5–29

⁵Now Rebekah was listening when Isaac spoke to his son Esau. So when Esau went to the field to hunt for game and bring it, ⁶Rebekah said to her son Jacob, "I heard your father say to your brother Esau, ⁷'Bring me game, and prepare for me savory food to eat, that I may bless you before the LORD before I die.' ⁸Now therefore, my son, obey my word as I command you. ⁹Go to the flock, and get me two choice kids, so that I may prepare from them savory food for your father, such as he likes; ¹⁰and you shall take it to your father to eat, so that he may bless you before he dies." ¹¹But Jacob said to his mother Rebekah, "Look, my brother Esau is a hairy man, and I am a man of smooth skin. ¹²Perhaps my father will feel me, and I shall seem to be mocking him, and bring a curse on myself and not a blessing." ¹³His mother said to him, "Let your curse be on me, my son; only obey my word, and go, get them for me." ¹⁴So he went and got them and

brought them to his mother; and his mother prepared savory food, such as his father loved. ¹⁵Then Rebekah took the best garments of her elder son Esau, which were with her in the house, and put them on her younger son Jacob; ¹⁶and she put the skins of the kids on his hands and on the smooth part of his neck. ¹⁷Then she handed the savory food, and the bread that she had prepared, to her son Jacob.

¹⁸So he went in to his father, and said, "My father"; and he said, "Here I am; who are you, my son?" ¹⁹Jacob said to his father, "I am Esau your firstborn. I have done as you told me; now sit up and eat of my game, so that you may bless me." ²⁰But Isaac said to his son, "How is it that you have found it so quickly, my son?" He answered, "Because the LORD your God granted me success." ²¹Then Isaac said to Jacob, "Come near, that I may feel you, my son, to know whether you are really my son Esau or not." ²²So Jacob went up to his father Isaac, who felt him and said, "The voice is Jacob's voice, but the hands are the hands of Esau." ²³He did not recognize him, because his hands were hairy like his brother Esau's hands; so he blessed him. ²⁴He said, "Are you really my son Esau?" He answered, "I am." ²⁵Then he said, "Bring it to me, that I may eat of my son's game and bless you." So he brought it to him, and he ate; and he brought him wine, and he drank. ²⁶Then his father Isaac said to him, "Come near and kiss me, my son." ²⁷So he came near and kissed him; and he smelled the smell of his garments, and blessed him, and said,

"Ah, the smell of my son
is like the smell of a field that the LORD has blessed.
²⁸May God give you of the dew of heaven,
and of the fatness of the earth,
and plenty of grain and wine.
²⁹Let peoples serve you,
and nations bow down to you.
Be lord over your brothers,
and may your mother's sons bow down to you.
Cursed be everyone who curses you,
and blessed be everyone who blesses you!"

Continue seeking the significance of this matriarchal text through the tradition and wisdom of Israel.

Without Rebekah's shrewd and decisive intervention, the conventional inheritance by the firstborn would prevail and Esau would receive the blessing of his blind and fading father. This final blessing of the father is unconditional and anoints the leader of the next generation of the family. In the biblical world, words spoken by authoritative persons have real substance and the capacity to shape the future. Since God had elected the younger son Jacob, Rebekah knows she must act quickly to mediate her family's destiny.

Mustering all in her power to seize the future, Rebekah is determined to achieve her goal. Knowing that she would be unable to convince Isaac to bless Jacob instead of Esau, she decides to trick her husband and to persuade Jacob to cooperate with her plan. When the hesitant Jacob raises the possibility of disastrous consequences, Rebekah takes the consequences of the scheme on her own shoulders and is willing to risk the curse for the well-being of her precious son (vv. 12–13). As the dramatic scene unfolds, Isaac is duped into bestowing the patriarchal blessing on his younger son Jacob.

Some commentators have described Rebekah's deception as immoral and dishonorable. Yet, the biblical world often valued craftiness in the underdog. Women often negotiated their way through patriarchal systems with shrewd ingenuity, and the powerless made their way in the world through clever trickery. Rebekah used whatever she could find in the tool kit of the disadvantaged, for Jacob's future and the birth oracle offered divine authority for her action.

The blessing assures agricultural fertility and prosperity (v. 28) as well as political domination and primacy for its recipient (v. 29). Through Rebekah's clever ruse, God again counters human presumption and turns usual expectation upside down, saying that "the elder shall serve the younger" (25:23). Because God's purposes are not explained, the narrative invites the listener to marvel rather than understand.

Answer this question to review this tense account of deception:

✝ Note how each of the senses is involved in the narrative: sight, hearing, smell, taste, and touch. Though Isaac's sight is failing, what indicates that his other senses are still acute?

Meditatio

Spend some time reflecting on the implications of this account of Rebekah's mediation of God's will for Jacob.

‡ Some commentators believe that Isaac was truly duped by the trick of Rebekah and Jacob; others suggest that he realized what was happening but went along with it, perhaps relieved that he didn't have to make the choice himself. What might be some indicators for each argument?

‡ What is admirable about Rebekah's use of trickery to obtain the blessing for Jacob? In what ways might the powerless and disadvantaged of our day resort to crafty deceit to make their way in a world controlled by wealth and power?

‡ By internalizing the blessings of our parents' love, we gain the self-esteem and confidence we need to make our way in the world. In what ways have I felt blessed or specially chosen by a parent or parent figures in my life?

Oratio

Speak to God in response to the words, ideas, and images from the reading. Use these or similar words.

> God of the past, present, and future, you empowered Rebekah to care for your will in the next generation of her family. Give me the insight and love necessary to bless the next generation with self-esteem and confidence. Help me to mediate your plan for the world through the hope you offer me.

Continue praying to God, through the guidance of God's Spirit . . .

Contemplatio

Realize that you have been blessed and chosen by God. Spend some quiet moments basking in God's parental love for you. Allow God's blessing to slowly permeate your entire being.

Write a few words summarizing your contemplative experience of being blessed by God.

Operatio

In what way could I bless or empower someone for the sake of the next generation?

17

Rebekah Rescues Jacob and Sends Him Away

Lectio

Continue listening to this narrative of Rebekah in which she saves the life of her son and prepares him for the future.

GENESIS 27:41–28:5

⁴¹Now Esau hated Jacob because of the blessing with which his father had blessed him, and Esau said to himself, "The days of mourning for my father are approaching; then I will kill my brother Jacob." ⁴²But the words of her elder son Esau were told to Rebekah; so she sent and called her younger son Jacob and said to him, "Your brother Esau is consoling himself by planning to kill you. ⁴³Now therefore, my son, obey my voice; flee at once to my brother Laban in Haran, ⁴⁴and stay with him a while, until your brother's fury turns away— ⁴⁵until your brother's anger against you turns away, and he forgets what you have done to him; then I will send, and bring you back from there. Why should I lose both of you in one day?"

⁴⁶Then Rebekah said to Isaac, "I am weary of my life because of the Hittite women. If Jacob marries one of the Hittite women such as these, one of the women of the land, what good will my life be to me?"

¹Then Isaac called Jacob and blessed him, and charged him, "You shall not marry one of the Canaanite women. ²Go at once to Paddan-

aram to the house of Bethuel, your mother's father; and take as wife from there one of the daughters of Laban, your mother's brother. ³May God Almighty bless you and make you fruitful and numerous, that you may become a company of peoples. ⁴May he give to you the blessing of Abraham, to you and to your offspring with you, so that you may take possession of the land where you now live as an alien— land that God gave to Abraham." ⁵Thus Isaac sent Jacob away; and he went to Paddan-aram, to Laban son of Bethuel the Aramean, the brother of Rebekah, Jacob's and Esau's mother.

After imaginatively listening to this narrative, continue seeking to understand its meaning through the following commentary.

Rebekah is shown to be consistently decisive and steadfast. When it came time to wed, she left her homeland for a new life. When she was in agony during her pregnancy, she inquired of God and received the crucial oracle about her sons. When it was time for Isaac to pass on his blessing to the next generation, she intervened in the way she judged best. Time after time Rebekah assessed the situation in faith, decided what to do, and took responsibility for her actions for the sake of her family's future. In this narrative, she again takes decisive action on behalf of her son's safety and future.

Hearing of Esau's vengeful desire to murder Jacob, Rebekah devises another strategy to protect her son. She instructs Jacob to flee to the home of her brother Laban in order to find sanctuary. She anticipates that Esau's anger will eventually cool, and when it is safe again, she will send word for Jacob to return home (vv. 43–45). Rebekah emphasizes her warning by expressing her fears of losing both sons in one day, for if Esau were to murder Jacob he would have to flee to escape the blood vengeance that would be exacted for his deed. Little did she realize that the bearer of God's promises would remain a fugitive for twenty years.

Rebekah's conversation with Isaac reveals a further motive for sending Jacob away. She desires that her favored son find a wife within the family circle. In order to convince Isaac to send Jacob, she points out how irritated the Hittite wives of Esau make her and how unbearable her life would be should Jacob too marry a woman from among the local peoples. Her plea persuades Isaac to call his son and offer him instructions and a blessing for his journey.

Isaac sends Jacob to the house of his maternal grandfather in Mesopotamia, giving his son a strict command not to intermarry with the women of the land of Canaan. The prohibition against intermarrying with other cultures would be strictly enforced for all the children of Israel in future generations in order to maintain the identity of the Israelites and the purity of their faith. Then Isaac blesses Jacob, asking God to give him the blessings given to Abraham, that he may be fruitful and his descendants numerous and that he may take possession of the Promised Land.

As matriarch of Israel, Rebekah devoted her life to the promises God gave to Abraham. She made the same journey from Mesopotamia that Sarah and Abraham had undertaken. Now she wants her own successor, the future matriarch and wife of Jacob, to carry out that same journey. Having secured for Jacob both the patriarchal blessing and the assurance that his wife would come from her own lineage, Rebekah disappears from the biblical narrative.

Sarah and Rebekah, the mothers of Israel's faith, are alike in many ways. Both play a crucial role in determining the future for their children. They act as God's mediators and partners in carrying out the divine will and passing on God's blessings. The two matriarchs each determine the success of their sons, often against the inclinations of their husbands. Their assertiveness corresponds to the lives of so many biblical women who, in the midst of patriarchal culture, exercise enormous power and influence within their families and households.

After carefully reading the Scripture and commentary, answer these questions:

✝ What are Rebekah's two motives for sending Jacob to her homeland?

✝ In what sense is Rebekah called the mother of Israel?

Meditatio

Spend some time reflecting on the text, asking yourself what personal message the passage has for you.

✝ What persuasion and diplomacy did Rebekah use with Isaac and with Jacob? How does this indicate the real power and influence of women within the Bible's ancient culture?

✝ Isaac's prohibition to Jacob not to marry a Canaanite forbids intermarriage with any people not under the bond and discipline of the covenant. What are some of the concerns today about marrying a person of another belief or religion?

✝ The life of Rebekah is colorful and admirable. What would I like to learn and remember from her life?

Oratio

Realizing that God has blessed you and given you an eternal inheritance, pray to God with a grateful heart.

God of our fathers and mothers, you call each generation to learn from the past and carry a legacy into the future. Rebekah served as your partner in carrying out your will and promises. May I always cultivate your promises and pass on the legacy of faith to future generations.

Continue responding to God with words generated by your reflection on the Scripture . . .

Contemplatio

Imagine yourself embraced by God, your loving parent. If this is a comfortable image for you, rest in God's tender arms and let your heart be filled with gratitude for his goodness and love.

Write a brief note about experiencing God as an affectionate parent.

Operatio

What do I know about the spiritual legacy handed down to me from previous generations in my family? What can I do to impart the best parts of that legacy to the next generation of my family?

18

Rebekah's Son Meets Rachel at the Well

Ask the Holy Spirit to guide your reading and help you discern the Word of God in this encounter at the well.

GENESIS 29:1–14

¹Then Jacob went on his journey, and came to the land of the people of the east. ²As he looked, he saw a well in the field and three flocks of sheep lying there beside it; for out of that well the flocks were watered. The stone on the well's mouth was large, ³and when all the flocks were gathered there, the shepherds would roll the stone from the mouth of the well, and water the sheep, and put the stone back in its place on the mouth of the well.

⁴Jacob said to them, "My brothers, where do you come from?" They said, "We are from Haran." ⁵He said to them, "Do you know Laban son of Nahor?" They said, "We do." ⁶He said to them, "Is it well with him?" "Yes," they replied, "and here is his daughter Rachel, coming with the sheep." ⁷He said, "Look, it is still broad daylight; it is not time for the animals to be gathered together. Water the sheep, and go, pasture them." ⁸But they said, "We cannot until all the flocks

are gathered together, and the stone is rolled from the mouth of the well; then we water the sheep."

⁹While he was still speaking with them, Rachel came with her father's sheep; for she kept them. ¹⁰Now when Jacob saw Rachel, the daughter of his mother's brother Laban, and the sheep of his mother's brother Laban, Jacob went up and rolled the stone from the well's mouth, and watered the flock of his mother's brother Laban. ¹¹Then Jacob kissed Rachel, and wept aloud. ¹²And Jacob told Rachel that he was her father's kinsman, and that he was Rebekah's son; and she ran and told her father.

¹³When Laban heard the news about his sister's son Jacob, he ran to meet him; he embraced him and kissed him, and brought him to his house. Jacob told Laban all these things, ¹⁴and Laban said to him, "Surely you are my bone and my flesh!" And he stayed with him a month.

Continue listening for the richer meaning of this narrative.

Though we hear no more of Rebekah, it is her plan that has brought Jacob to Mesopotamia. In a narrative resembling the scene a generation earlier with the young Rebekah at a well outside Haran, here we learn the result of Rebekah's desire for her son Jacob to find a spouse from among her kin. Again, a well is the backdrop for the introduction of a future matriarch. The primary concern of the account is the transmission of God's promises to the next generation of Israel's patriarchs and matriarchs.

The local well is a primary meeting place for shepherds, and throughout the Bible, it is the place where love begins to blossom. Three flocks of sheep are waiting to be watered there when Jacob arrives. A huge stone covers the opening of the well, protecting the purity of the water. Each day, when several shepherds have gathered at the well, they roll away the stone, water their flocks, and return the stone to its place.

When Jacob learns from the shepherds that they are from Haran, he inquires about Laban, the brother of Rebekah. They point to a young woman who is leading a flock to the well and tell him that she is Laban's daughter Rachel. When Jacob sees her against the desert sky, he knows that she is his heart's destiny. Elated by her presence, he rolls away the massive stone by himself and graciously gives water to her sheep. Overjoyed, he kisses Rachel and begins to weep. When Jacob tells Rachel that he is the son of Rebekah, she runs home to tell the news to her father.

Though the scene resembles the earlier encounter between the young Rebekah and Abraham's servant, there are significant differences. The servant had an impressive train of camels, bearing gifts for the bride and her family. Jacob arrives as a fugitive with nothing to offer but his own strength and labor. Abraham's servant tested Rebekah's suitability to be Isaac's bride by waiting for her to draw water for him and his camels. Here it is Jacob who must prove his own suitability by drawing water for the flock.

On hearing Rachel's report, Laban runs to the well to meet his nephew. His greeting and welcome of Jacob are marked by a moving display of family affection. Yet, we also recall that this is the same Laban who, as a young man, had a greedy eye for personal profit when he saw the great riches borne by Abraham's servant. When he embraces Jacob, he hails him as a kindred spirit: "Surely you are my bone and my flesh!" (v. 14). We shouldn't fail to see the irony when these two tricksters, Laban and Jacob, meet. The kiss of kinship and affection will soon show itself to be a deception as Laban's self-interest comes to the fore. But Jacob's headlong love for Rachel will blind him to the intrigues at work in this distant land.

After listening for the Word of God in this text, try to answer the following questions:

‡ What are the primary similarities between the scenes of the young Rebekah (Gen. 24:10–33) and of Rachel at the well?

‡ What are the most notable differences between the two scenes?

Meditatio

Spend some time meditating on this story of Rachel's first encounter with Jacob.

✝ The well is a feminine sexual symbol in ancient literature. The closed well represents Rachel's virgin sexuality, and Jacob's removal of the stone expresses the beginning of her sexual awareness. What are some of the emotions that might have been felt by Rachel and Jacob at this first encounter?

✝ Jacob's love and his need for love create an emotional blindness within him. In what ways can love and our need for love blind us to what might otherwise seem obvious?

✝ The Word of God has been compared to a deep well full of refreshing water that never goes stale. No matter how many times we dip into the well of sacred Scripture, there is always more refreshing water to drink. In what way have I experienced the truth of this ancient metaphor?

Oratio

Pray to God through the Holy Spirit in whatever way seems to respond to the divine Word spoken to you through this text.

> God of our ancestors, you brought the fleeing Jacob to the well to heal his heart with love. May I recognize within the waters of this well the power to transform my life. Help me to draw forth the renewing gifts of your divine Spirit so that I can offer your presence to others and so renew my life in you.

Continue praying using the biblical images from this passage . . .

Contemplatio

The Word of God is like a deep well from which refreshing waters may be drawn. Spend a few moments in grateful contemplation, realizing that God has blessed you with the quenching waters of sacred Scripture to refresh your spirit.

Write a few words from your contemplative experience.

Operatio

How might I more effectively make use of God's refreshing Word to restore and energize my spirit? How can I allow God to renew my life today?

19

Leah and Rachel Married to Jacob

Lectio

Vocalize the words of this intriguing text so that you not only read with your eyes but also hear with your ears. Read and listen carefully for God's Word to you.

GENESIS 29:15–30

¹⁵Then Laban said to Jacob, "Because you are my kinsman, should you therefore serve me for nothing? Tell me, what shall your wages be?" ¹⁶Now Laban had two daughters; the name of the elder was Leah, and the name of the younger was Rachel. ¹⁷Leah's eyes were lovely, and Rachel was graceful and beautiful. ¹⁸Jacob loved Rachel; so he said, "I will serve you seven years for your younger daughter Rachel." ¹⁹Laban said, "It is better that I give her to you than that I should give her to any other man; stay with me." ²⁰So Jacob served seven years for Rachel, and they seemed to him but a few days because of the love he had for her.

²¹Then Jacob said to Laban, "Give me my wife that I may go in to her, for my time is completed." ²²So Laban gathered together all the people of the place, and made a feast. ²³But in the evening he took his daughter Leah and brought her to Jacob; and he went in to her.

²⁴(Laban gave his maid Zilpah to his daughter Leah to be her maid.) ²⁵When morning came, it was Leah! And Jacob said to Laban, "What is this you have done to me? Did I not serve with you for Rachel? Why then have you deceived me?" ²⁶Laban said, "This is not done in our country—giving the younger before the firstborn. ²⁷Complete the week of this one, and we will give you the other also in return for serving me another seven years." ²⁸Jacob did so, and completed her week; then Laban gave him his daughter Rachel as a wife. ²⁹(Laban gave his maid Bilhah to his daughter Rachel to be her maid.) ³⁰So Jacob went in to Rachel also, and he loved Rachel more than Leah. He served Laban for another seven years.

Continue seeking the significance of this narrative in God's plans to bless his people.

During this brief sketch of fourteen years, all the characters in the drama are introduced. We learn that Laban has two daughters—Leah is the "elder" and Rachel is the "younger" (v. 16). Their description recalls the description of Rebekah's two sons, Esau the elder and Jacob the younger. Leah, whose name means "cow," is described as having lovely eyes. Another word for this uncertain description of her eyes is "tender," perhaps a reference to her inner compassion in contrast to her outward plainness. Rachel, whose name means "ewe lamb," is said to be "graceful and beautiful" (v. 17). She is loved by Jacob, who is willing to do anything to have her as his bride. In every way, Leah suffers by comparison with her sister. Though Rachel seems to be favored, we will see that God favors Leah and blesses her with abundant fertility. Like Hagar in the stories of Abraham, Leah is the unloved one who is cared for by God. We are also introduced to Zilpah, the maid of Leah, and Bilhah, the maid of Rachel. Their introductions raise our curiosity by causing us to wonder about their future role in this complicated family system and to look toward the next episode.

Laban, always eager for a profit, recognizes Jacob's fondness for Rachel and his ability to manipulate him. Laban shrewdly asks Jacob to set his own wages, knowing that Jacob's youth and his love will prompt him to suggest a compensation favorable to Laban. Jacob eagerly accepts and proposes that he work seven years as the bride price for Rachel. Laban's response is a study in evasion. He seems to agree to Jacob's proposal but promises nothing (v. 19). Jacob, however, motivated by anticipation and love, hears a promise of Rachel and eagerly works for seven years.

When the seventh year ends, Jacob is filled with longing and demands his wife. Laban replies by preparing a great wedding feast. When evening comes, Laban takes his older daughter, heavily veiled as is the custom, into the marriage chamber. In the light of day, Jacob discovers that he has married Leah instead of Rachel: "When morning came, it was Leah!" (v. 25). The marriage, consummated through the sexual pleasures of the night, cannot be repudiated. Jacob the deceiver has been deceived. Laban has used the darkness to fool Jacob, just as Jacob used the darkness of Isaac's blindness to dupe him. Forced to depend on their less reliable senses, both men were duped as they closed their eyes to the deception being worked upon them. The crafty Jacob, who switched places with his older brother to gain the blessing, has been deceived by the switch of younger and older sisters. When Jacob states his case to Laban and demands to know why he was deceived, Laban says simply, "This is not done in our country—giving the younger before the firstborn" (v. 26).

Laban's words sting Jacob. Ever since his struggle with Esau in Rebekah's womb, the rights of the firstborn have obstructed Jacob's way. Here the preference for the elder impedes Jacob's love for Rachel just as it had earlier hindered his inheritance. Leah is the older, so Rachel must wait. This time Jacob does not have his mother to help him and has no deceptive trick to reverse the order. Jacob has met his match in his uncle Laban, who deceives him out of fourteen years of his life. So Jacob must wait. Just as in the lives of his ancestors, God will keep his promises, but those promised blessings are delayed year after long year.

Try to answer this question after listening to the text and reading its commentary:

‡ What is the irony in the reversal of the younger and the older sister?

Meditatio

Reflect on your own understanding of this narrative of Leah and Rachel. Repeat and ponder whatever words or phrases strike you from your reading.

† The text gives little or no indication of how Leah and Rachel felt about their father's deception of Jacob. How might each daughter have emotionally responded to the situation?

† Many women, like Leah, are married to men who love someone or something more than their wives. What are some of these substitute loves that occur in marriage today?

† Beneath the human intrigue of this scene, God is working for the good. In what way is the theme of divine inversion at work in this passage? When have I experienced disappointment, only to discover that God has a better way than my own?

Oratio

After reflecting on this treacherous scene, respond in prayer using the language of Scripture.

God of faithful and compassionate love, only in hindsight are your people able to see the fullness of your blessings. In the midst of the frustrations and disappointments of my life, help me to know that you are at work to bring about the good.

Continue praying to the One who reverses the expectations of the world . . .

Contemplatio

Imagine yourself as either Leah or Rachel. In the midst of life's ups and downs, be still and relax in God's unconditional love for you.

Write a few words from your silent contemplation before the living God.

Operatio

Beneath the rivalry of Leah and Rachel is the struggle for self-image. What increases my self-esteem? What can I do to better my self-image?

20

Leah, Bilhah, and Zilpah Give Birth

Listen to this account of childbirth and let it draw you into the heart of God.
Note any words or phrases that strike you in a new way.

GENESIS 29:31–30:13

³¹When the LORD saw that Leah was unloved, he opened her womb; but Rachel was barren. ³²Leah conceived and bore a son, and she named him Reuben; for she said, "Because the LORD has looked on my affliction; surely now my husband will love me." ³³She conceived again and bore a son, and said, "Because the LORD has heard that I am hated, he has given me this son also"; and she named him Simeon. ³⁴Again she conceived and bore a son, and said, "Now this time my husband will be joined to me, because I have borne him three sons"; therefore he was named Levi. ³⁵She conceived again and bore a son, and said, "This time I will praise the LORD"; therefore she named him Judah; then she ceased bearing.

¹When Rachel saw that she bore Jacob no children, she envied her sister; and she said to Jacob, "Give me children, or I shall die!" ²Jacob became very angry with Rachel and said, "Am I in the place of God, who has withheld from you the fruit of the womb?" ³Then

she said, "Here is my maid Bilhah; go in to her, that she may bear upon my knees and that I too may have children through her." ⁴So she gave him her maid Bilhah as a wife; and Jacob went in to her. ⁵And Bilhah conceived and bore Jacob a son. ⁶Then Rachel said, "God has judged me, and has also heard my voice and given me a son"; therefore she named him Dan. ⁷Rachel's maid Bilhah conceived again and bore Jacob a second son. ⁸Then Rachel said, "With mighty wrestlings I have wrestled with my sister, and have prevailed"; so she named him Naphtali.

⁹When Leah saw that she had ceased bearing children, she took her maid Zilpah and gave her to Jacob as a wife. ¹⁰Then Leah's maid Zilpah bore Jacob a son. ¹¹And Leah said, "Good fortune!" so she named him Gad. ¹²Leah's maid Zilpah bore Jacob a second son. ¹³And Leah said, "Happy am I! For the women will call me happy"; so she named him Asher.

Enhance your understanding of this narrative through the interpretation offered here.

God looks upon Leah, the unloved and undesired one, and blesses her with children, while Rachel, the loved and desired one, remains barren. Each woman is deprived of what she wants the most and tormented with jealousy by what the other possesses. The two sisters have been set against each other by their greedy and manipulative father. He has deprived his daughters of happiness to gain the service of a son-in-law.

Because Leah is the fertile wife, she gains a secure and respected status in her family. Yet, she is emotionally bereft. Overshadowed by her beautiful, younger sister, she desperately desires the love and attention of her husband. She hopes in vain that by bearing children for Jacob she will win his love. The names of her children express her yearning for her husband's affection and something about the texture of her relationship with God.

Rachel is beautiful and graceful to behold, and she is adored by her husband. Though she was chosen by Jacob as his wife, her wedding bed was usurped by her sister. Not only must she suffer the humiliation of sharing her husband, she also must bear the disgrace of infertility. No matter how intensely Jacob loves her, she cannot conceive. Since children are a family's most valued asset, failing to become a mother is its darkest shame. With each child Leah bears, Rachel's misery increases.

Distressed by her barrenness and jealous of her sister, who has already borne four sons, Rachel lashes out at Jacob and demands that he give her children (v. 1). Jacob responds sharply, deflecting the blame, and acknowledges that the future of their family is in the hands of God (v. 2). In desperation, Rachel decides to offer her maid Bilhah to Jacob as a surrogate. Through the same legal procedure followed by her barren ancestor Sarah, Rachel would have children and build up her own family. Bilhah bears two sons for Rachel, whom the latter adopts into her own family. Leah also enters the competition out of jealousy. Since she has ceased bearing children, she offers her maid Zilpah to Jacob. Zilpah has two sons for Leah, whom she also adopts into her own family. Their names indicate that her children, not Jacob, are the center of her life.

Leah and Rachel express a broad but familiar range of female experiences. One is beautiful, the other plain. One is fertile, the other barren. One expresses the image of the lover, the other of the mother. Each is unhappy because she craves what the other possesses. Neither can appreciate her own distinctive qualities because she is so preoccupied with the other's perceived advantages. Neither is able to feel whole because she continually measures herself against others who seem to have it all. They are stuck in comparison, competition, and self-contempt. The story of Leah and Rachel challenges all women to appreciate their own unique qualities, to be flexible and forgiving of self, and to appreciate God's many blessings.

After hearing the words of the biblical text and its commentary, try to respond to these questions:

✢ What does Leah have that Rachel covets?

✢ What does Rachel have that Leah covets?

Meditatio

Consider the ways in which this narrative of marital relationships, childbirth, and family dynamics is reflected in your own experiences.

‡ What aspects of Jacob's family do I recognize in my own family? Competition? Jealousy? Conflicts?

‡ In the Bible, most polygamous marriages experience deep and bitter conflicts. What are the primary problems with multiple spouses, as indicated in the account of Leah and Rachel?

‡ Why are Leah and Rachel so unhappy when they seem blessed?

Oratio

Speak to God in response to the words, ideas, and images of your reading. Offer to God what you have discovered about yourself from your meditation.

Lord God, you blessed Leah and Rachel with the gifts of beauty, fertility, children, and love. Teach me to rid my life of comparison, competition, and self-contempt. Help me to appreciate my uniqueness and the many ways my life has been blessed by you.

Continue pouring out your prayer to God until words are no longer necessary or useful . . .

Contemplatio

Consider your most important qualities and your most significant gifts. Take some time to nurture your grateful heart in the presence of your generous God.

Write a few words about your experience of focused contemplatio.

Operatio

How would my life be different if I stopped comparing myself unfavorably to others? What steps can I take to develop a greater appreciation of my own blessed uniqueness?

21

Faithful Commitments
Fulfilled for Rachel

Read this narrative carefully and be open to the new insights and encouragement God is offering you.

GENESIS 30:14–24

¹⁴In the days of wheat harvest Reuben went and found mandrakes in the field, and brought them to his mother Leah. Then Rachel said to Leah, "Please give me some of your son's mandrakes." ¹⁵But she said to her, "Is it a small matter that you have taken away my husband? Would you take away my son's mandrakes also?" Rachel said, "Then he may lie with you tonight for your son's mandrakes." ¹⁶When Jacob came from the field in the evening, Leah went out to meet him, and said, "You must come in to me; for I have hired you with my son's mandrakes." So he lay with her that night. ¹⁷And God heeded Leah, and she conceived and bore Jacob a fifth son. ¹⁸Leah said, "God has given me my hire because I gave my maid to my husband"; so she named him Issachar. ¹⁹And Leah conceived again, and she bore Jacob a sixth son. ²⁰Then Leah said, "God has endowed me with a good dowry; now my husband will honor me, because I have borne

him six sons"; so she named him Zebulun. [21]Afterwards she bore a daughter, and named her Dinah.

[22]Then God remembered Rachel, and God heeded her and opened her womb. [23]She conceived and bore a son, and said, "God has taken away my reproach"; [24]and she named him Joseph, saying, "May the LORD add to me another son!"

Continue listening for the understanding and guidance this text can offer you.

The stories of Israel's ancestors continue to offer us a complex display of the intricacies of family life. No matter how quickly Jacob hurries between the tents of his wives and their maids, he will never be able to satisfy all their emotional needs. Polygamy doesn't seem to work very well in the families of the Bible. Trust and intimacy can flourish only between two people. When a third enters the relationship, suspicion, jealously, and anger soon supplant love's harmony.

In her increasingly desperate struggle to have children, Rachel discovers that Leah's oldest son has found some mandrakes while harvesting wheat and has brought them to his mother. Mandrakes are fruit that grow wild in the fields and were known in the ancient world as an aphrodisiac and fertility enhancer. When Rachel politely asks Leah for some of the fruit in hopes that it might help her to conceive, Leah sarcastically accuses Rachel of taking away her husband. Then, taking advantage of Rachel's desire for children, Leah strikes a rather pathetic bargain to exchange a night with Jacob for the mandrakes. When Jacob comes in from the fields that evening, Leah informs him of the arrangement, and he seems to readily agree. Ironically, Leah, who gives up the mandrakes, becomes pregnant again, while Rachel, who possesses the fruit, remains barren until Leah has borne three more children. The narrator emphasizes that new life is in the hands of God and cannot be controlled by human manipulation.

The entire narrative concerning the children of Leah and the barrenness of Rachel has awaited its climax: God remembers Rachel, God hears her cry, and God opens her womb (v. 22). God is the subject of the action. God acts on Rachel's behalf in light of his past promises and present fidelity.

Rachel bears her child, not because of any surrogate maids or fertility potions but because of God's mercy.

Leah has borne six sons and one daughter of her own and two sons through Zilpah. Rachel's shame is taken away with the birth of Joseph. She has borne two sons through Bilhah and one of her own. Joseph's name expresses Rachel's hope of having another child and anticipates the final chapter of Rachel's life. Jacob now has eleven sons, and the important twelfth son has not yet been born. The narrative lays the foundation of Israel's twelve-tribe system, so critically significant for the ongoing history of God's people in the Promised Land.

The birth of Rachel's son Joseph coincides with the end of Jacob's obligations toward Laban. God's promises of numerous offspring have been generously fulfilled, and Joseph's birth from Jacob's favored wife motivates Jacob to want to return to his native land. The transformation wrought in Rachel through childbirth is the catalyst for further change in Jacob. Both have learned to love, which will lead to reconciliation within his family. Another turning point in the narrative of this chosen family has been reached, and Jacob knows he must find a way to bring his wives and children home.

After listening to this anxious narrative of conceptions and births, try to answer these questions:

✝ What seems to be the effectiveness of the mandrakes in this narrative?

✝ Why did Rachel finally bear a child after so much waiting?

Meditatio

*Reflect on the narrative of this text as if it were a story told to you. Allow the
words to affirm your role in the family of God and your unique contribution.*

✝ What problems result when relationships form a triangle of trouble?
How can committed couples avoid such dilemmas?

✝ How do human beings mediate their instinctive drives toward polygamy?
What are some of the cultural and emotional motives for monogamy?

✝ What is different about the description of Dinah, the daughter of Leah,
in comparison to the narrative of each son? What does this suggest about
the role of daughters in the ancient world?

Oratio

Respond to God's Word to you with your own words to God. Speak from your heart in response to the hope you have been offered.

Faithful God, you remember your people and respond to their cries in every age. As you fulfilled your promises to Rachel, express your commitment to me as I call to you in my need. Hear my prayer and come to my assistance.

Continue to express your hopes, desires, struggles, and commitment ...

Contemplatio

Though you sit alone, realize that you are a part of the family of God. Consider your conception and birth from the perspective of your all-loving God. Contemplate the joy of God as he calls you by name into his family.

Write a few words about the feelings that fill your heart.

Operatio

What hopes and expectations do I cultivate for my life? How can I transform vague hopes into confident expectations as I consider God's desires for me?

22

Rachel and Leah
Leave Their Homeland

Lectio

*Read aloud this narrative in which God calls the family of Jacob to leave
Mesopotamia and travel to Canaan. Consider the social challenges of hearing and obeying God's call.*

GENESIS 31:13–35

[13]"I am the God of Bethel, where you anointed a pillar and made
a vow to me. Now leave this land at once and return to the land of
your birth." [14]Then Rachel and Leah answered him, "Is there any
portion or inheritance left to us in our father's house? [15]Are we not
regarded by him as foreigners? For he has sold us, and he has been
using up the money given for us. [16]All the property that God has taken
away from our father belongs to us and to our children; now then,
do whatever God has said to you."

[17]So Jacob arose, and set his children and his wives on camels; [18]and
he drove away all his livestock, all the property that he had gained,
the livestock in his possession that he had acquired in Paddan-aram,
to go to his father Isaac in the land of Canaan.

[19]Now Laban had gone to shear his sheep, and Rachel stole her
father's household gods. [20]And Jacob deceived Laban the Aramean,
in that he did not tell him that he intended to flee. [21]So he fled with

all that he had; starting out he crossed the Euphrates, and set his face toward the hill country of Gilead.

²²On the third day Laban was told that Jacob had fled. ²³So he took his kinsfolk with him and pursued him for seven days until he caught up with him in the hill country of Gilead. ²⁴But God came to Laban the Aramean in a dream by night, and said to him, "Take heed that you say not a word to Jacob, either good or bad."

²⁵Laban overtook Jacob. Now Jacob had pitched his tent in the hill country, and Laban with his kinsfolk camped in the hill country of Gilead. ²⁶Laban said to Jacob, "What have you done? You have deceived me, and carried away my daughters like captives of the sword. ²⁷Why did you flee secretly and deceive me and not tell me? I would have sent you away with mirth and songs, with tambourine and lyre. ²⁸And why did you not permit me to kiss my sons and my daughters farewell? What you have done is foolish. ²⁹It is in my power to do you harm; but the God of your father spoke to me last night, saying, 'Take heed that you speak to Jacob neither good nor bad.' ³⁰Even though you had to go because you longed greatly for your father's house, why did you steal my gods?" ³¹Jacob answered Laban, "Because I was afraid, for I thought that you would take your daughters from me by force. ³²But anyone with whom you find your gods shall not live. In the presence of our kinsfolk, point out what I have that is yours, and take it." Now Jacob did not know that Rachel had stolen the gods.

³³So Laban went into Jacob's tent, and into Leah's tent, and into the tent of the two maids, but he did not find them. And he went out of Leah's tent, and entered Rachel's. ³⁴Now Rachel had taken the household gods and put them in the camel's saddle, and sat on them. Laban felt all about in the tent, but did not find them. ³⁵And she said to her father, "Let not my lord be angry that I cannot rise before you, for the way of women is upon me." So he searched, but did not find the household gods.

After reading this inspired narrative, continue listening for God's Word and seeking a deeper understanding.

After Jacob has been with his father-in-law, Laban, for twenty years, God reveals to him that the time has come to return to his homeland. Rachel and Leah, like Sarah and Rebekah before them, agree to leave their native land

and journey to Canaan. These two rival sisters wholeheartedly consent to travel with Jacob, since they know their father has treated them more as foreigners than as family (vv. 13–16). They feel as though Laban has sold them rather than building up an inheritance for their families. Deprived by Laban of their rightful share of the family's wealth, they consider that whatever goods and livestock Jacob had acquired from their father now belongs to them and their children.

Jacob's life has come full circle. As he fled from his homeland to Mesopotamia at the direction of his mother, Rebekah, many years before (27:43), he now flees from Mesopotamia to his homeland with Rachel and Leah, Bilhah and Zilpah, and his twelve children. Jacob chose the annual event of sheep shearing, the springtime occasion during which Laban and his sons would be away and preoccupied, as his opportunity for departure.

Rachel takes advantage of her father's absence to steal the household gods, small statues of the deities that were thought to bring protection, good fortune, and fertility. Her motive is unclear from the text. She may be acting in spite against her father or belittling the power of the gods to help him. Since the possessor of the household gods in Mesopotamia was said to be the leader of the family, Rachel is perhaps removing the symbols of Laban's authority and laying claim to the inheritance for her own son Joseph.

When Laban is told that his daughters and grandchildren have fled, he pursues them and overtakes them near the land of Canaan. Told in a dream not to take hostile action against Jacob, Laban accuses him of foolishly taking his daughters as well as his household gods. Out of fear of Laban's reprisal, Jacob admits that he has taken his wives, but unaware that Rachel had taken the statues, he pledges that the culprit will die. His assurance portends Rachel's early death.

Rachel has hidden the household gods in her camel's saddle. When Laban searches from tent to tent, he is unable to find them. Coming to Rachel's tent, he finds her sitting on the saddle. Rachel explains that she is unable to get up when he enters because of her menstrual period. Whether true or not, her excuse is a willful defilement of the statues and a vivid depiction of the narrator's scorn for the idols. Rachel has proven herself clever in deceiving her male relatives just as her mother-in-law, Rebekah, had done.

Meditatio

Reflect on the text and seek its more personal meaning and significance.

✝ What grievances do Rachel and Leah harbor against their father (vv. 14–16)? How do men treat women in comparable ways today?

✝ What seems to be the most likely reason for Rachel's theft of her father's household gods? What does this narrative say about the power of such gods through the playful contrast of the God of Jacob and the gods of Laban?

✝ Trapped within their father's family, Rachel and Leah are bound and treated unjustly. Their escape to Canaan alludes to the later exodus of their descendants from the bondage of Egypt. What are some of the parallels between this passage and Exodus?

Oratio

Give praise and thanks to God for the gift of freedom. Speak words that express whatever new hope or purpose you have discovered in this Scripture.

> Lord God, you desire freedom and abundant life for all your people. Just as you led the families of Rachel and Leah as they fled from their bondage and traveled to the Promised Land, lead me with your power and guidance on the journey to freedom and new life.

Continue to express your prayer to God with a heart full of faith . . .

Contemplatio

Be still, realizing that God persistently calls you out of bondage and into freedom. Be grateful for the new life of freedom that God continually offers you.

Write a few words about the gratitude you feel.

Operatio

When have I found new freedom through forgiveness or reconciliation? What can I do to free my life from the bondage of unresolved grievances against another?

23

The Rape of Dinah

Lectio

Read this tale of terror with eyes and ears open to understand its meaning within the context of the biblical narrative of our ancestors.

GENESIS 34:1–31

¹Now Dinah the daughter of Leah, whom she had borne to Jacob, went out to visit the women of the region. ²When Shechem son of Hamor the Hivite, prince of the region, saw her, he seized her and lay with her by force. ³And his soul was drawn to Dinah daughter of Jacob; he loved the girl, and spoke tenderly to her. ⁴So Shechem spoke to his father Hamor, saying, "Get me this girl to be my wife."

⁵Now Jacob heard that Shechem had defiled his daughter Dinah; but his sons were with his cattle in the field, so Jacob held his peace until they came. ⁶And Hamor the father of Shechem went out to Jacob to speak with him, ⁷just as the sons of Jacob came in from the field. When they heard of it, the men were indignant and very angry, because he had committed an outrage in Israel by lying with Jacob's daughter, for such a thing ought not to be done.

⁸But Hamor spoke with them, saying, "The heart of my son Shechem longs for your daughter; please give her to him in marriage. ⁹Make marriages with us; give your daughters to us, and take our daughters for yourselves. ¹⁰You shall live with us; and the land shall

be open to you; live and trade in it, and get property in it." ¹¹Shechem also said to her father and to her brothers, "Let me find favor with you, and whatever you say to me I will give. ¹²Put the marriage present and gift as high as you like, and I will give whatever you ask me; only give me the girl to be my wife."

¹³The sons of Jacob answered Shechem and his father Hamor deceitfully, because he had defiled their sister Dinah. ¹⁴They said to them, "We cannot do this thing, to give our sister to one who is uncircumcised, for that would be a disgrace to us. ¹⁵Only on this condition will we consent to you: that you will become as we are and every male among you be circumcised. ¹⁶Then we will give our daughters to you, and we will take your daughters for ourselves, and we will live among you and become one people. ¹⁷But if you will not listen to us and be circumcised, then we will take our daughter and be gone."

¹⁸Their words pleased Hamor and Hamor's son Shechem. ¹⁹And the young man did not delay to do the thing, because he was delighted with Jacob's daughter. Now he was the most honored of all his family. ²⁰So Hamor and his son Shechem came to the gate of their city and spoke to the men of their city, saying, ²¹"These people are friendly with us; let them live in the land and trade in it, for the land is large enough for them; let us take their daughters in marriage, and let us give them our daughters. ²²Only on this condition will they agree to live among us, to become one people: that every male among us be circumcised as they are circumcised. ²³Will not their livestock, their property, and all their animals be ours? Only let us agree with them, and they will live among us." ²⁴And all who went out of the city gate heeded Hamor and his son Shechem; and every male was circumcised, all who went out of the gate of his city.

²⁵On the third day, when they were still in pain, two of the sons of Jacob, Simeon and Levi, Dinah's brothers, took their swords and came against the city unawares, and killed all the males. ²⁶They killed Hamor and his son Shechem with the sword, and took Dinah out of Shechem's house, and went away. ²⁷And the other sons of Jacob came upon the slain, and plundered the city, because their sister had been defiled. ²⁸They took their flocks and their herds, their donkeys, and whatever was in the city and in the field. ²⁹All their wealth, all their little ones and their wives, all that was in the houses, they captured and made their prey. ³⁰Then Jacob said to Simeon and Levi, "You

have brought trouble on me by making me odious to the inhabitants of the land, the Canaanites and the Perizzites; my numbers are few, and if they gather themselves against me and attack me, I shall be destroyed, both I and my household." [31]But they said, "Should our sister be treated like a whore?"

Continue struggling to understand the full implications of this Scripture through the following remarks:

Dinah is the daughter of Leah, the only daughter of Jacob named. Her story is a tale of terror, of men's passion and power, of violent violation and vengeance. Dinah's feelings and desires are never disclosed. Her nightmare begins with a seemingly harmless deed: "Dinah . . . went out to visit the women of the region" (v. 1). Shechem, the prince of the region, seizes her and lays with her by force. After his disgraceful deed, he is enamored of her and desires her for his wife, all the while keeping her captive in his house.

When Dinah's brothers hear of Shechem's deed, they are incensed at the "outrage" (v. 7). Shechem and his father propose that the two peoples enter into alliance involving intermarriage and commerce, and they offer to pay a high bridal price for Dinah. The sons of Jacob respond "deceitfully" because of the defilement of their sister, demanding that all the males of the city be circumcised before entering such an agreement (vv. 13–17). Shechem is immediately circumcised and persuades the whole city to accept the painful ritual, assuring them that intermarriage with the family of Jacob would be economically advantageous (vv. 18–24).

As the men of the city are still in pain and incapacitated, the sons of Jacob carry out their treacherous plan. Simeon and Levi, sons of Leah and full brothers of Dinah, slay all the men of the city and rescue Dinah, while their other brothers plunder the city. Jacob himself disapproves of his sons' ruthless actions out of fear of being hated by all the peoples of the land, but the brothers of Dinah consider their actions deeds of reprisal for the dishonor done to their sister (vv. 25–31).

Meditatio

*After hearing this ancient narrative, spend some time considering its signifi-
cance. Bring your insights to bear on the following questions:*

‡ What might account for the difference between the mild response of Jacob
to his daughter's abduction and the passionate response of his sons? How
does this story demonstrate how violence begets violence?

‡ Notice that Shechem's dialogue with Jacob and his sons never mentions
the disgrace he inflicted on Dinah. What seem to be the primary concerns
of the men in this negotiation? How might this have been different if
Dinah and her mother were involved in the discussion?

‡ Intermarriage of the sons of Jacob among the people of the land of
Canaan would, over time, result in the loss of their identity and distinctiveness as the seed of Abraham and inheritors of God's promise.
In what way are faith and belief important considerations in marriage
between two people?

Oratio

Respond in prayer to your interaction with this text.

> God of the covenant, Dinah was violated, captured, and silenced by a culture opposed to your covenant. Motivate us to rescue women held in sexual and economic bondage throughout your world today. Help us reflect your compassionate and liberating will.

Continue this prayer in words that issue from your heart . . .

Contemplatio

Consider the suffering of women held in bondage throughout the world today. In silence, let God deepen your concern and compassion for them so that you reflect God's loving heart.

Write a few words about your contemplative experience.

Operatio

What can I do to find out about oppressed and suffering women today? What can I do to help their cause?

24

Deborah and Rachel
Die along the Journey

Lectio

Put away the distractions of the day and enter a quiet place where you can hear God's voice speaking to you through the words of Scripture. Ask the Holy Spirit to fill your heart as you read.

GENESIS 35:6–20

⁶Jacob came to Luz (that is, Bethel), which is in the land of Canaan, he and all the people who were with him, ⁷and there he built an altar and called the place El-bethel, because it was there that God had revealed himself to him when he fled from his brother. ⁸And Deborah, Rebekah's nurse, died, and she was buried under an oak below Bethel. So it was called Allon-bacuth.

⁹God appeared to Jacob again when he came from Paddan-aram, and he blessed him. ¹⁰God said to him, "Your name is Jacob; no longer shall you be called Jacob, but Israel shall be your name." So he was called Israel. ¹¹God said to him, "I am God Almighty: be fruitful and multiply; a nation and a company of nations shall come from you, and kings shall spring from you. ¹²The land that I gave to Abraham and Isaac I will give to you, and I will give the land to your offspring

after you." ¹³Then God went up from him at the place where he had spoken with him. ¹⁴Jacob set up a pillar in the place where he had spoken with him, a pillar of stone; and he poured out a drink offering on it, and poured oil on it. ¹⁵So Jacob called the place where God had spoken with him Bethel.

¹⁶Then they journeyed from Bethel; and when they were still some distance from Ephrath, Rachel was in childbirth, and she had hard labor. ¹⁷When she was in her hard labor, the midwife said to her, "Do not be afraid; for now you will have another son." ¹⁸As her soul was departing (for she died), she named him Ben-oni; but his father called him Benjamin. ¹⁹So Rachel died, and she was buried on the way to Ephrath (that is, Bethlehem), ²⁰and Jacob set up a pillar at her grave; it is the pillar of Rachel's tomb, which is there to this day.

After listening to this narrative of death and remembrance, continue seeking its meaning through the scholarship and tradition of Israel.

Having reentered the land of God's promise, Jacob follows in the footsteps of Abraham and Sarah from Shechem to Bethel. Here Jacob has returned to the place where God appeared to him many years before as he was fleeing from his brother Esau at Rebekah's insistence. He builds an altar at Bethel in commemoration of God's faithful guidance during his years outside the land of Canaan. As God appears to Jacob again, he changes his name to Israel and blesses him and his family with the blessings given to Abraham and Sarah. His family will be so fruitful that they will become a great nation, the people of Israel will settle in the land, and great kings will come from them (vv. 10–12). With eleven sons and at least one daughter, Jacob's family is well on its way.

Here Deborah, the nurse of Rebekah, dies and is buried under an oak tree that came to be called Allon-bacuth, meaning "the oak of weeping" (v. 8). She must have spent many years with Rebekah, caring for her needs as well as those of her twins. The report of her death brings closure to Jacob's relationship with his mother, who had devised the scheme by which Jacob had fled from Canaan to spend much of his life in Mesopotamia. The narrator must have been familiar with other traditions about Deborah that have been lost to us that would have made this notice of her death understandable. The Jewish rabbinical tradition has speculated that Rebekah sent Deborah to Jacob in Mesopotamia to fulfill her promise to send for Jacob after Esau's anger subsided (27:45). Apparently Rebekah died while Jacob was away, but no account of her death is included in the Torah. The report about Deborah, her nurse, compensates in some measure for the absence of an account of Rebekah's burial and the need to honor the end of this matriarch's life in the Scriptures of Israel. In attending to the burial of Deborah and honoring her at Bethel, Jacob mourns his mother and participates at least vicariously in her burial and memorializing.

As Jacob's family travels on, Rachel is stricken with severe birth pangs as she gives birth to another son. Her longing for another child is finally fulfilled but at the cost of her life (vv. 16–17). As Rachel is dying, she names her son Ben-oni, "son of my sorrow," but knowing the importance of a name in defining one's life and destiny, Jacob renames him Benjamin, "son of my right hand" (v. 18). Perhaps this name honors Rachel as Jacob's right hand, his most important partner.

Rachel is buried beside the road leading to Ephrath, which is interpreted to mean Bethlehem (v. 19). Jacob reveals the great honor in which he held Rachel by setting up a pillar over her tomb, giving her an everlasting memorial in the Promised Land (v. 20). Just as that monument to Rachel was seen by all who passed by in the days of the ancestors, it is still seen by pilgrims today along the road leading into Bethlehem.

After hearing this text and its commentary, answer these questions:

✢ Why might the writer have made special note of the death of Deborah in the Genesis text?

✢ Why is it appropriate that Jacob's name be changed to Israel at the time Rachel gives birth to his twelfth son?

Meditatio

After thinking about the meaning of this text, reflect on its impact in your own life. Bringing God's Word into the present context of your life, spend some time meditating on these questions:

✝ Like Deborah, the nurse of Rebekah, many women help families with the tasks of raising children: relatives, friends, day care workers, teachers, medical personnel, and others. What women have I known who fulfilled these tasks? For which of these women in my own life do I weep? Which do I remember?

✝ The birth of Benjamin and the death of Rachel demonstrate the intergenerational faith of this family. What events have reminded me that family life is a combination of sorrow and celebration and that death moves on to new life?

✝ In what ways do tombs, graves, or memorials move me to experience renewed life even while I'm reminded of death and sorrow?

Oratio

You have listened to this account of suffering, death, and new life. Now respond to God in the context of your own life with the words of Scripture and the words of your heart.

Ever-faithful God, when Rachel, the mother of your people, died, she was memorialized by her family. Help me to remember and honor those people who have led me to you and helped me to experience richer life.

Continue speaking to God, giving voice to the feelings within your heart . . .

Contemplatio

Places like Bethel, Allon-bacuth, and Rachel's tomb memorialize deep sorrow and new life for the family of Jacob. Consider a place that is a similar memorial for you. Imagine yourself in that location and rest there in silence, asking God to make his presence known to you.

Write a few words that arise from your contemplative experience of God's presence.

Operatio

What can I do to honor or memorialize a deceased loved one in a way that is significant? Which of that person's qualities do I wish to incorporate into my own life?

25

Tamar, the
Righteous Woman

As you listen to this narrative, consider why many believe it is told from a woman's point of view. Ask God to guide your reading with his own Spirit.

GENESIS 38:6–30

⁶Judah took a wife for Er his firstborn; her name was Tamar. ⁷But Er, Judah's firstborn, was wicked in the sight of the LORD, and the LORD put him to death. ⁸Then Judah said to Onan, "Go in to your brother's wife and perform the duty of a brother-in-law to her; raise up offspring for your brother." ⁹But since Onan knew that the offspring would not be his, he spilled his semen on the ground whenever he went in to his brother's wife, so that he would not give offspring to his brother. ¹⁰What he did was displeasing in the sight of the LORD, and he put him to death also. ¹¹Then Judah said to his daughter-in-law Tamar, "Remain a widow in your father's house until my son Shelah grows up" —for he feared that he too would die, like his brothers. So Tamar went to live in her father's house.

¹²In course of time the wife of Judah, Shua's daughter, died; when Judah's time of mourning was over, he went up to Timnah to his sheep-shearers, he and his friend Hirah the Adullamite. ¹³When Tamar was

told, "Your father-in-law is going up to Timnah to shear his sheep," [14]she put off her widow's garments, put on a veil, wrapped herself up, and sat down at the entrance to Enaim, which is on the road to Timnah. She saw that Shelah was grown up, yet she had not been given to him in marriage. [15]When Judah saw her, he thought her to be a prostitute, for she had covered her face. [16]He went over to her at the road side, and said, "Come, let me come in to you," for he did not know that she was his daughter-in-law. She said, "What will you give me, that you may come in to me?" [17]He answered, "I will send you a kid from the flock." And she said, "Only if you give me a pledge, until you send it." [18]He said, "What pledge shall I give you?" She replied, "Your signet and your cord, and the staff that is in your hand." So he gave them to her, and went in to her, and she conceived by him. [19]Then she got up and went away, and taking off her veil she put on the garments of her widowhood. [20]When Judah sent the kid by his friend the Adullamite, to recover the pledge from the woman, he could not find her. [21]He asked the townspeople, "Where is the temple prostitute who was at Enaim by the wayside?" But they said, "No prostitute has been here." [22]So he returned to Judah, and said, "I have not found her; moreover the townspeople said, 'No prostitute has been here.'" [23]Judah replied, "Let her keep the things as her own, otherwise we will be laughed at; you see, I sent this kid, and you could not find her."

[24]About three months later Judah was told, "Your daughter-in-law Tamar has played the whore; moreover she is pregnant as a result of whoredom." And Judah said, "Bring her out, and let her be burned." [25]As she was being brought out, she sent word to her father-in-law, "It was the owner of these who made me pregnant." And she said, "Take note, please, whose these are, the signet and the cord and the staff." [26]Then Judah acknowledged them and said, "She is more in the right than I, since I did not give her to my son Shelah." And he did not lie with her again.

[27]When the time of her delivery came, there were twins in her womb. [28]While she was in labor, one put out a hand; and the midwife took and bound on his hand a crimson thread, saying, "This one came out first." [29]But just then he drew back his hand, and out came his brother; and she said, "What a breach you have made for yourself!" Therefore he was named Perez. [30]Afterward his brother came out with the crimson thread on his hand; and he was named Zerah.

Continue seeking the motives of this honorable woman as you understand the story in its ancient context.

When Judah's first son died before having children with Tamar, Judah followed his obligation of giving her in marriage to his second son to raise up children for his dead brother. When this son rejected his responsibility, knowing that a son for Tamar would reduce the inheritance of his own children, he died in punishment for refusing to give an heir for his deceased brother. Judah then promised Tamar to his third son when he came of age to marry. Yet, fearing that this last son would also die after marriage to Tamar, he delayed the marriage indefinitely. By being dishonest about his intentions, Judah wronged Tamar and trapped her in a hopeless state.

Still under the jurisdiction of Judah's family, Tamar takes matters into her own hands and deceives Judah in order to achieve justice and protect her future. She ceases to be a victim, hatching a successful plot to conceive a child with Judah. When Judah hears that Tamar has acted as a prostitute and is pregnant, he orders that she be brought out and burned to death (v. 24). Yet, Tamar holds the upper hand and conducts herself calmly and forthrightly, showing the seal, cord, and staff, which identify Judah as the one responsible for her pregnancy.

The climax of the story comes with Judah's shocked and humbled response, saying of Tamar, "She is more in the right than I" (v. 26). Tamar has acted out of the highest motives by having a child within the family of Judah. She has honored the demands of her relationship with her deceased husband, whereas Judah has not. By taking unconventional risks and humbling herself in order to hold Judah accountable, she is judged more honorable and maintains the line of Judah.

Like her ancestors, Sarah and Rebekah, Tamar refuses to wait on men. She uses the power she possesses to see God's will accomplished as she understands it. Tamar gives birth to twins, two new sons for Judah after the death of his first two sons. Her bold initiative and willingness to risk scandal, humiliation, and death make it possible for the family of Judah to thrive and develop into the future kingdom of Judah. Despite Judah's weakness, God's saving plan is not frustrated. This woman Judah would have put to death will become the ancestor of the royal tribe from which King David will ascend.

Meditatio

Consider what significance this passage has for the history of salvation and for your own place within it.

✝ The laws of Israel, in the context of the ancient world, were protective of women and their dignity. What might be the advantages of the ancient law mandating a childless woman's marriage to the brother of her deceased husband (see Deut. 25:5–10)?

✝ Tamar honors her responsibility to bear a child as an heir to her late husband. In what way does her risky and courageous action result in a glorious future for her family? Why is Tamar the first woman mentioned in the New Testament (Matt. 1:3)?

✝ What was Judah's response to his discovery that Tamar was pregnant? Was it a double standard for him to condemn her actions but not his own? Do such double standards still exist today?

Oratio

Who are the female figures you want to lift up in joyful thanksgiving for their lives? Respond in prayer to your meditation on the life of Tamar.

> Lord God, you preserved the family of Judah through the assertive acts of a Canaanite woman. I praise you for the ways you bring good out of painful and tragic events. Give me the courage and assertive strength of Tamar to provide what you will for my family and their future.

Continue to pray in whatever words arise from your own heart . . .

Contemplatio

After words are no longer useful in prayer, just rest silently in the heart and arms of your loving God. Know that God is giving you whatever daring and confidence you need to claim your future.

Write a few words that linger from your silent time in God's presence.

Operatio

What brave women do I remember from my family's past? What helps me to be courageous for the sake of my family and future?

26

Joseph and the Egyptian Wife of Potiphar

Read this account aloud so that you can both see and hear this narrative. Try to imagine the scene as you read.

GENESIS 39:1–23

¹Now Joseph was taken down to Egypt, and Potiphar, an officer of Pharaoh, the captain of the guard, an Egyptian, bought him from the Ishmaelites who had brought him down there. ²The LORD was with Joseph, and he became a successful man; he was in the house of his Egyptian master. ³His master saw that the LORD was with him, and that the LORD caused all that he did to prosper in his hands. ⁴So Joseph found favor in his sight and attended him; he made him overseer of his house and put him in charge of all that he had. ⁵From the time that he made him overseer in his house and over all that he had, the LORD blessed the Egyptian's house for Joseph's sake; the blessing of the LORD was on all that he had, in house and field. ⁶So he left all that he had in Joseph's charge; and, with him there, he had no concern for anything but the food that he ate.

Now Joseph was handsome and good-looking. ⁷And after a time his master's wife cast her eyes on Joseph and said, "Lie with me."

⁸But he refused and said to his master's wife, "Look, with me here, my master has no concern about anything in the house, and he has put everything that he has in my hand. ⁹He is not greater in this house than I am, nor has he kept back anything from me except yourself, because you are his wife. How then could I do this great wickedness, and sin against God?" ¹⁰And although she spoke to Joseph day after day, he would not consent to lie beside her or to be with her. ¹¹One day, however, when he went into the house to do his work, and while no one else was in the house, ¹²she caught hold of his garment, saying, "Lie with me!" But he left his garment in her hand, and fled and ran outside. ¹³When she saw that he had left his garment in her hand and had fled outside, ¹⁴she called out to the members of her household and said to them, "See, my husband has brought among us a Hebrew to insult us! He came in to me to lie with me, and I cried out with a loud voice; ¹⁵and when he heard me raise my voice and cry out, he left his garment beside me, and fled outside." ¹⁶Then she kept his garment by her until his master came home, ¹⁷and she told him the same story, saying, "The Hebrew servant, whom you have brought among us, came in to me to insult me; ¹⁸but as soon as I raised my voice and cried out, he left his garment beside me, and fled outside."

¹⁹When his master heard the words that his wife spoke to him, saying, "This is the way your servant treated me," he became enraged. ²⁰And Joseph's master took him and put him into the prison, the place where the king's prisoners were confined; he remained there in prison. ²¹But the LORD was with Joseph and showed him steadfast love; he gave him favor in the sight of the chief jailer. ²²The chief jailer committed to Joseph's care all the prisoners who were in the prison, and whatever was done there, he was the one who did it. ²³The chief jailer paid no heed to anything that was in Joseph's care, because the LORD was with him; and whatever he did, the LORD made it prosper.

Continue listening for the meaning and significance of this text in God's saving plan.

Joseph was the son of Jacob and Rachel. His mother died when he was young, and he was his father's favorite child. As his mother was "graceful and beautiful" (29:17), Joseph was "handsome and good-looking" (v. 6).

He was a constant reminder to Jacob of his beloved wife Rachel and was hated by his brothers. When they sold Joseph into slavery, he was taken to Egypt and served in the household of Potiphar. There he became successful and won the confidence and esteem of his Egyptian master. From the outset and at the end of the narrative, God is shown to be the unseen force directing Joseph's success, causing all that he did to prosper (vv. 3, 23).

Not all the strong women of the Bible use their power for good purposes. The infamous and unnamed wife of Potiphar abuses her position for her self-serving desires. Aware of Joseph's status as a slave, she brazenly commands him to lie with her. But Joseph, at great risk to his own safety, repeatedly declines her overtures out of loyalty to her husband and devotion to God (vv. 8–10). When she fails in one last attempt, her rage and desire for revenge lead her to denounce Joseph to her household and her husband. She accuses Joseph of leaving his garment behind after attempting to rape her. When Potiphar hears her accusation, he is enraged and sends Joseph to prison. The fact that he does not have Joseph put to death may hint either that Joseph defended himself convincingly or that Potiphar doubted the veracity of his wife's story.

Despite being sold into slavery by his brothers and being falsely accused by his master's wife, Joseph knows that God is with him and will not abandon him. He refuses to forsake the covenant that his mother and father instilled in him from an early age. After Potiphar's wife succeeds in having Joseph punished and put in jail, she vanishes from the narrative. Her deceitful actions become the means for Joseph's even higher ascent within Potiphar's house. His imprisonment becomes the instrument of his rise to the second highest position in the land of Egypt. Because of Joseph's loyalty to God's covenant, he transcends his position as slave and prisoner, foreshadowing the movement of God's covenanted people from the age of the patriarchs and matriarchs to the period of enslavement and subsequent liberation under Moses.

Conclude your study of this narrative by answering this question:

‡ What is the reason for Joseph's success, both in Potiphar's house and in prison?

Meditatio

Consider what you can learn from the interactions between Joseph and Potiphar's wife.

⸸ The advantages given to Joseph by his mother, Rachel, were nearly cancelled by the temptations he experienced in his success. In what ways are successful young musicians and athletes today tempted by their celebrity and achievements?

⸸ In what ways are adversities necessary to temper our advantages? How has adversity given me the resilience necessary for life's challenges?

⸸ Parents often find it difficult to watch their children struggle without rushing to their rescue. Why do children and young people need to experience hardship in order to grow?

Oratio

Speak to God in response to your reflection on this passage. Pray to the One who knows you intimately, cares about you deeply, and accepts you unconditionally.

> Giver of all good gifts, I know that receiving what I want is not necessarily a blessing. I intuitively understand that experiencing hardship and disappointment is often the way to fuller life. Help me to trust in your promises when I feel frustrated, and keep me confident in your plan in the midst of adversity.

Continue speaking to God in whatever ways seem to respond to the divine Word spoken to you . . .

Contemplatio

When Joseph experienced enslavement, he remembered the faith of his mother, Rachel. When he was imprisoned, he recalled God's covenant that she had taught him. Rest quietly in the covenant promises of God and trust that God has your best interests at heart.

Write a few words about your contemplative experience.

Operatio

Joseph was successful because God was with him and caused all that he did to prosper. What would my life be like if I truly believed that about myself?

27

Midwives and Daughters
Save God's People

Lectio

*Kiss the words of the biblical text and ask God to let these inspired words speak
to your spirit today. Honor the women of Egypt as you listen to these verses.*

EXODUS 1:15–22; 2:1–10

¹⁵The king of Egypt said to the Hebrew midwives, one of whom was
named Shiphrah and the other Puah, ¹⁶"When you act as midwives to
the Hebrew women, and see them on the birthstool, if it is a boy, kill
him; but if it is a girl, she shall live." ¹⁷But the midwives feared God;
they did not do as the king of Egypt commanded them, but they let
the boys live. ¹⁸So the king of Egypt summoned the midwives and
said to them, "Why have you done this, and allowed the boys to live?"
¹⁹The midwives said to Pharaoh, "Because the Hebrew women are not
like the Egyptian women; for they are vigorous and give birth before
the midwife comes to them." ²⁰So God dealt well with the midwives;
and the people multiplied and became very strong. ²¹And because the
midwives feared God, he gave them families. ²²Then Pharaoh commanded all his people, "Every boy that is born to the Hebrews you
shall throw into the Nile, but you shall let every girl live."

¹Now a man from the house of Levi went and married a Levite
woman. ²The woman conceived and bore a son; and when she saw

that he was a fine baby, she hid him three months. [3]When she could hide him no longer she got a papyrus basket for him, and plastered it with bitumen and pitch; she put the child in it and placed it among the reeds on the bank of the river. [4]His sister stood at a distance, to see what would happen to him.

[5]The daughter of Pharaoh came down to bathe at the river, while her attendants walked beside the river. She saw the basket among the reeds and sent her maid to bring it. [6]When she opened it, she saw the child. He was crying, and she took pity on him, "This must be one of the Hebrews' children," she said. [7]Then his sister said to Pharaoh's daughter, "Shall I go and get you a nurse from the Hebrew women to nurse the child for you?" [8]Pharaoh's daughter said to her, "Yes." So the girl went and called the child's mother. [9]Pharaoh's daughter said to her, "Take this child and nurse it for me, and I will give you your wages." So the woman took the child and nursed it. [10]When the child grew up, she brought him to Pharaoh's daughter, and she took him as her son. She named him Moses, "because," she said, "I drew him out of the water."

After reading this passage with your mind and heart, continue listening to the inspired text through these comments:

As in the book of Genesis, women continue to determine the course of events in the book of Exodus. These heroic women—the midwives, Moses's mother and sister, Pharaoh's daughter and her maids—are the saviors of early Israel and begin the process of their liberation from Egyptian slavery.

As Exodus begins, the new king of Egypt is seeking to contain the Israelites with harsh labor, but the more they are oppressed the more they multiply and flourish. Then he orders that all the male babies be put to death by the midwives as they are born. Ironically, he chooses professional life bearers to be his instruments of death. In a courageous act of civil disobedience, the Hebrew midwives, Shiphrah and Puah, defy his orders. Because they fear God, they become channels of life for God's people as the nation of Israel is being born.

Pharaoh's orders to kill the infant boys and let the girls live presumes that females pose no threat to his oppressive power. This male-oriented perspective becomes laughable as the women become the prime agents to undermine his policy. Two powerless midwives resist the commands of Egypt's king, and God rewards them with children of their own. Indeed, all the Hebrew women are said to be vigorous and lively in giving birth. A potential death story abounds in birth and life, as the Hebrew people multiply and become strong in the land.

When the king of Egypt orders that every boy be thrown into the Nile while the girls may live, the mothers and daughters of the land subvert his command. The women do for the infant Moses what God will do for the Hebrew people. Moses's mother refuses to kill at Pharaoh's command and instead puts her child in a basket among the reeds of the river in an attempt to save his life. The daughter of Pharaoh sees the child of the oppressed Hebrews in the river and is moved with pity. Moses's sister brings together his biological mother and his adoptive mother in an ironic conspiracy that results in the life of the child. Through the combined efforts of these women, Moses is rescued so that he can become the instrument of God's liberation of Israel from Egypt.

The combined work of these women not only protects the child but also reunites him with his mother. In an amazing twist, the daughter of Pharaoh not only agrees to accept the baby's mother as his nurse but also decides to pay her funds from Egypt's royal treasury to nurse her own son. Then Pharaoh's daughter adopts Moses as her son and assures his education in the very court from which he will deliver his people.

After seeking to understand the implications of the women's conspiracy, answer these questions:

✝ Why did Pharaoh let the girls live? What does this say about him?

✝ At what part of this story of their past would the people of Israel laugh most heartily?

Meditatio

Ask yourself how God is speaking to you in this passage and what his message means for your own life.

‡ What kinds of questions and fears faced these women as they pondered their acts of civil disobedience against the court of Pharaoh?

‡ Why did the mother of Moses give her child up for adoption? What risks did the daughter of Pharaoh take in order to adopt this child of the Hebrews? What similar issues do parents face today in the process of adoption?

‡ The death-dealing policies of Pharaoh are countered by the life-enhancing work of the women in this narrative. In what ways do women today struggle against oppressive systems and institutions?

Oratio

Pray with trust and confidence in whatever way God gives to you as a result of his grace.

Lord our God, you are always calling your people forth from bondage and oppression to freedom and new life. Help me participate in your redeeming power by working for justice and human rights. Give me inspiration through the women of Israel and confidence in your empowering Spirit.

Continue to pray in response to the Word you have heard . . .

Contemplatio

God has adopted you and made you his own child. Believe that the God who knows you through and through also loves you beyond measure. Rest in the loving arms of your divine parent.

Write a few words that linger from your silent time in God's presence.

Operatio

The life-giving work of the women stands in sharp contrast to the death-dealing policies of Pharaoh. In what ways can I promote a culture of life in the midst of the counter-trends of our society today?

28

Zipporah, the Wife of Moses

Lectio

Listen to these accounts from the adult life of Moses. Try to understand what God wishes to communicate to you through these ancient texts.

EXODUS 2:15–22; 4:19–26

¹⁵But Moses fled from Pharaoh. He settled in the land of Midian, and sat down by a well. ¹⁶The priest of Midian had seven daughters. They came to draw water, and filled the troughs to water their father's flock. ¹⁷But some shepherds came and drove them away. Moses got up and came to their defense and watered their flock. ¹⁸When they returned to their father Reuel, he said, "How is it that you have come back so soon today?" ¹⁹They said, "An Egyptian helped us against the shepherds; he even drew water for us and watered the flock." ²⁰He said to his daughters, "Where is he? Why did you leave the man? Invite him to break bread." ²¹Moses agreed to stay with the man, and he gave Moses his daughter Zipporah in marriage. ²²She bore a son, and he named him Gershom; for he said, "I have been an alien residing in a foreign land."

¹⁹The Lord said to Moses in Midian, "Go back to Egypt; for all those who were seeking your life are dead." ²⁰So Moses took his wife and his sons, put them on a donkey and went back to the land of Egypt; and Moses carried the staff of God in his hand.

²¹And the LORD said to Moses, "When you go back to Egypt, see that you perform before Pharaoh all the wonders that I have put in your power; but I will harden his heart, so that he will not let the people go. ²²Then you shall say to Pharaoh, 'Thus says the LORD: Israel is my firstborn son. ²³I said to you, "Let my son go that he may worship me." But you refused to let him go; now I will kill your firstborn son.'"

²⁴On the way, at a place where they spent the night, the LORD met him and tried to kill him. ²⁵But Zipporah took a flint and cut off her son's foreskin, and touched Moses' feet with it, and said, "Truly you are a bridegroom of blood to me!" ²⁶So he let him alone. It was then she said, "A bridegroom of blood by circumcision."

Continue to listen to this Scripture from the book of Exodus through the following commentary.

As Moses fled from Egypt as a young man, he came to the land of the Midianites, a nomadic people living in the desert region of Sinai. Here, as in the tradition of Isaac and Rebekah as well as Jacob and Rachel, Moses meets his future wife at a well. The seven young women who come to draw water for their father's flock are introduced as the daughters of Reuel, the priest of Midian. When they are driven away by shepherds, Moses rescues them and waters their flock. His concern to free those treated unjustly anticipates his role in the exodus. The Midianite priest offers hospitality to Moses and gives him his daughter Zipporah in marriage. When she gives birth to their first son, Moses names him Gershom, which expresses Moses's experience as a stranger living away from home.

After the passage of many years, God instructs Moses to return to Egypt. He takes his wife and sons from their life in Midian and begins the journey back. Moses carries with him the staff of God, prefiguring the liberating work God will give him among his people. God's words to Moses, describing Israel as God's "firstborn son" (4:22), evoke the tenderness of a parent-child relationship. God's relationship with his people is a covenant of intimate love. The divine parent enters deeply into the pains of the suffering child to deliver her from suffering and bondage.

While Zipporah and Moses journey toward Egypt, God threatens the life of Moses. Due to the unusual circumstances of his upbringing, Moses had not been circumcised, the visible sign of his acceptance of God's covenant. If Moses is to lead God's people to freedom, he must accept circumcision for himself and his family. Acting quickly, Zipporah circumcises her son with a flint and then daubs the feet (probably a euphemism for genitals) of Moses with the bloody foreskin. In this cryptic scene, it seems that Zipporah's act of vicarious circumcision averts God's anger and preserves the life of Moses. Her incantation, "truly you are a bridegroom of blood to me!" (v. 25), harkens back to the early place of circumcision as a rite of puberty and preparation for marriage.

This is the only biblical account in which a woman performs the act of circumcision. But in performing this action, she delivers Moses from death, as Moses will deliver the Israelites. She becomes a mediator between God and her husband, as Moses will mediate between God and his people. When God sees the blood sacrifice and hears Zipporah's words, the threat of death subsides. The event prefigures Israel's night of liberation when, seeing the blood spread on the lintel and the doorposts, God will turn away the destroyer from the firstborn sons and bring his people into freedom and life.

Again, a woman has saved Moses from death and preserved God's plan to save Israel. Like the midwives, the mother and sister of Moses, and the daughter of Pharaoh, Zipporah is instrumental in continuing God's strategy to bring redemption to his people. These women stood up to political power, paternal power, and even divine power while perceptively knowing and assertively doing what needed to be done.

After listening carefully to these texts involving Zipporah, try to answer these questions:

‡ In what way does Moses's encounter with Zipporah at the well place this couple in the tradition of their ancestors from the book of Genesis?

‡ In what ways does God act as a tender parent to the children of Israel?

Meditatio

Ponder whatever words or phrases strike you most from your lectio. Reflect on how God is deepening your understanding and enriching your hope through these Scriptures.

✝ What characteristics do all these women of the book of Exodus have in common? What qualities do I admire most in them?

✝ Moses's rescue of the seven daughters of Reuel from the abusive shepherds demonstrates a character trait that he developed throughout his life. When have I noticed a passion for justice within myself?

✝ In the scene of Zipporah and Moses on their journey to Egypt, the redeeming quality of the spilled blood foreshadows the blood of the Pascal Lamb. What qualities of sacrificial blood do I notice throughout the Bible?

Oratio

Having listened to and reflected on God's Word to you in the Scripture text, now respond to God from your heart in prayer.

> God of justice and might, the women of Exodus developed a passion for justice and a determination to struggle against the political and social forces that threatened their families and their people. Give me the desire to courageously follow in their footsteps.

Continue praying in whatever words seem to express the content of your heart . . .

Contemplatio

Quietly place yourself in God's presence, and then ask God to give you the vision and courage to be a prophet of justice in the world. Allow your heart to be transformed with a passionate love for his people.

What words come to mind after your contemplative time in God's presence?

Operatio

What about these women of Exodus would I like to imitate? To what action am I drawn today after meditating on and praying over these Scriptures?

29

The Prophet Miriam Sings of God's Triumph

Read aloud these fragmentary texts about Miriam, the sister of Moses. Listen with your heart to the way God addresses you through these words.

EXODUS 15:19–21

[19]When the horses of Pharaoh with his chariots and his chariot drivers went into the sea, the LORD brought back the waters of the sea upon them; but the Israelites walked through the sea on dry ground.

[20]Then the prophet Miriam, Aaron's sister, took a tambourine in her hand; and all the women went out after her with tambourines and with dancing. [21]And Miriam sang to them:

"Sing to the LORD, for he has triumphed gloriously;
horse and rider he has thrown into the sea."

NUMBERS 12:1–9

[1]While they were at Hazeroth, Miriam and Aaron spoke against Moses because of the Cushite woman whom he had married (for he had indeed married a Cushite woman); [2]and they said, "Has the LORD

spoken only through Moses? Has he not spoken through us also?" And the LORD heard it. ³Now the man Moses was very humble, more so than anyone else on the face of the earth. ⁴Suddenly the LORD said to Moses, Aaron, and Miriam, "Come out, you three, to the tent of meeting." So the three of them came out. ⁵Then the LORD came down in a pillar of cloud, and stood at the entrance of the tent, and called Aaron and Miriam; and they both came forward. ⁶And he said, "Hear my words:

When there are prophets among you,
I the LORD make myself known to them in visions;
I speak to them in dreams.
⁷Not so with my servant Moses;
he is entrusted with all my house.
⁸With him I speak face to face—clearly, not in riddles;
and he beholds the form of the LORD.

Why then were you not afraid to speak against my servant Moses?" ⁹And the anger of the LORD was kindled against them, and he departed.

Continue searching for the meaning and significance of these texts within the tradition of Israel.

Through various texts scattered throughout the Hebrew Scriptures, Miriam emerges as a mediator, prophet, worship leader, and musician. At the beginning of Exodus, she is the young girl who brings together Pharaoh's daughter and Moses's mother. Serving as the mediator between the women of Egypt and the Hebrew women, Miriam saves Moses from death so that he can become the liberator of their people. Immediately after this great redemption from Egypt, Miriam leads the community in a celebration of victory through song and dance. In other texts, such as Micah 6:4, Israel remembers Miriam as one of the leaders of Israel in the wilderness period: "For I brought you up from the land of Egypt, and redeemed you from the house of slavery; and I sent before you Moses, Aaron, and Miriam."

Miriam's victory celebration praises God for Israel's victory at the sea. The ritual seems to be a liturgical action intended to help the people experience the event anew, to express its meaning for the people, and to keep it alive in the communal memory. The dramatic movements of dance, accompanied by the poetic words of the music and the sound of the tambourine, express the trepidation and ecstasy, the struggle and triumph, and God's conquest over oppression and death (v. 20–21). As a prophet, Miriam is a messenger of God, leading the people to understand their present experience and to imagine the future God wishes for them.

Israel's memory of Miriam as a leader in the wilderness community, alongside Moses and Aaron, is reflected in the book of Numbers. In this narrative, Miriam and Aaron confront Moses concerning their role in the leadership of the people. The first complaint involves the shift in family relationships brought about by Moses's wife (v. 1). Perhaps this wife had more influence with Moses than his siblings. Their primary grievance, however, emerges as they ask, "Has the LORD spoken only through Moses? Has he not spoken through us also?" (v. 2). They challenge Moses's role as the supreme channel of God's Word to the Israelites. As prophet and priest among the people, Miriam and Aaron feel they have legitimate claims as mediators of God's revelation.

God gathers the three leaders to the tent of meeting in order to speak to them (v. 4). God states that prophets have a legitimate role among the people because God speaks to them through dreams and visions. But God emphasizes the role of Moses as the one through whom God speaks in a direct, clear, and unmediated form. Through such intimacy with God, Moses reveals God's Word in an authoritative way like no other. The dispute among these three leaders reflects the tension that existed throughout Israel's history among the royal, prophetic, and priestly traditions of leadership among the people.

Having listened to these ancient texts, think about this question:

‡ What are the roles of Miriam among God's people as revealed in these passages?

Meditatio

Spend some time meditating on the words of the text you have read. Let God's Word touch your heart deeply and work to bring confidence to your spirit.

‡ Belonging to the people of Israel meant being a part of a people whom God had led in a marvelous passage from slavery and death to freedom and life. In what ways do I continue to sing, dance, and liturgically celebrate that reality?

‡ The complementary roles of shepherd, prophet, and priest experienced both healthy tension and damaging conflict throughout the tradition of Israel. Are there ways in which this tension is still present in the church today?

‡ Miriam experienced a call to prophetic leadership among the people. The scene of her conflict with Moses reflects a tension between traditional roles held by men and the genuine experiences of women in ministry. In what ways does this scene reflect such tensions today?

Oratio

Pray to God with praise and thanksgiving as the Spirit of God prompts you.

Victorious Lord, you have cast into the sea all the power of oppression that held your people in captivity. Help us to rejoice in the freedom you have won for us and give you thanks for the new life that is ours. Make me a minister of your continuing presence among us.

Continue to pour out your heart to God, who always hears your prayers . . .

Contemplatio

God is the Victor, the source of your freedom and life. Continue to worship God without words. Simply place yourself in humble adoration before him.

Write a few words to describe your time of contemplatio.

Operatio

In what way am I called to be a messenger or mediator of God's Word to others? What can I do to enhance my prophetic ministry?

30

Five Daughters Advocate
for Their Rights

Lectio

Listen carefully to God's message concerning these five obscure daughters in Israel's history. Consider how this revelation advanced Israel's understanding of God's will for women.

NUMBERS 27:1–11

¹Then the daughters of Zelophehad came forward. Zelophehad was son of Hepher son of Gilead son of Machir son of Manasseh son of Joseph, a member of the Manassite clans. The names of his daughters were: Mahlah, Noah, Hoglah, Milcah, and Tirzah. ²They stood before Moses, Eleazar the priest, the leaders, and all the congregation, at the entrance of the tent of meeting, and they said, ³"Our father died in the wilderness; he was not among the company of those who gathered themselves together against the LORD in the company of Korah, but died for his own sin; and he had no sons. ⁴Why should the name of our father be taken away from his clan because he had no son? Give to us a possession among our father's brothers."

⁵Moses brought their case before the LORD. ⁶And the LORD spoke to Moses, saying: ⁷The daughters of Zelophehad are right in what they

are saying; you shall indeed let them possess an inheritance among their father's brothers and pass the inheritance of their father on to them. [8]You shall also say to the Israelites, "If a man dies, and has no son, then you shall pass his inheritance on to his daughter. [9]If he has no daughter, then you shall give his inheritance to his brothers. [10]If he has no brothers, then you shall give his inheritance to his father's brothers. [11]And if his father has no brothers, then you shall give his inheritance to the nearest kinsman of his clan, and he shall possess it. It shall be for the Israelites a statute and ordinance, as the LORD commanded Moses."

After listening to the formation of this ancient legislation, continue seeking its fuller meaning and significance for communities of faith.

The names of these five daughters of Zelophehad are carefully preserved in the Torah because they refused to be erased from Israel's history. The women are remembered by name—Mahlah, Noah, Hoglah, Milcah, and Tirzah—because they stood up for themselves in the arena of inheritance rights, a field forever controlled by men. These five brought about change in the law by appealing to the foundational values of their tradition. Faithful to the God of the exodus, they acted not so much for themselves but for the good of their family, tribe, nation, and the whole tradition of God's people.

The five daring women appear before Moses claiming they should inherit their father's land. Ancient Israel had a patrilineal system of inheritance, whereby the land was passed from father to son and therefore kept within the family and tribe. But what if, as in the case of Zelophehad, a man died leaving only daughters and no sons? The five women had no male to represent them in the census of the nation that Moses ordered before reaching the land of Canaan. If their household went uncounted, they would receive no land after crossing the Jordan River into the land of promise. So the women assert that they should inherit the property so as to preserve their father's name on the land (v. 4).

Faced with this new situation, Moses goes to God for guidance and returns with a new inheritance law that champions the rights of daughters to their father's inheritance in the absence of sons: "If a man dies, and has no son, then you shall pass his inheritance on to his daughter" (v. 8). God sides with the five women, declaring that the land must remain in the family's possession, even if it means contradicting the regulation that only men can inherit the land.

The book of Numbers transitions from the fixed setting of Mount Sinai, where Moses received the unchangeable revelation of God for Israel, to the transportable tent of meeting. From this movable tabernacle, God promised to travel with the people and continue revealing the divine will as new circumstances arose. The tent of meeting invites ongoing dialogue between God and his people, and it represents the openness of revelation and the flexibility of Israel's tradition. God's Word is not an entrenched legalism but a living tradition that is both faithful to the past and receptive toward the future.

Mahlah, Noah, Hoglah, Milcah, and Tirzah are able to take one small step toward greater justice for women by challenging the practices of their times and appealing to the permanent values of their tradition. Though the underlying patriarchal system remains—the land will revert to their male husband upon marriage or at least to their male son upon their death— these five women serve as example and inspiration for those in every age concerned about the issues of justice and gender.

After reading this inspired text, synthesize your experience of lectio by answering these questions:

‡ How does the legislation of the Ten Commandments differ from the regulations established here?

‡ How can the revelation of God's will be both permanent and adaptable?

Meditatio

Enlightened by the example of these five women, consider your own under-
standing of their deed and its implications for your life.

✢ What offers me inspiration and hope from the narrative of these five
women? In what ways would I like to imitate their method and style of
advocacy?

✢ Under what circumstances would I be willing to challenge an established
law? How might I go about doing so?

✢ How can churches and communities be both traditional and progressive?
In what sense does the encounter described in this narrative maintain
both qualities?

Oratio

Respond with prayer to God after listening to him and reflecting on this passage. Ask for the wisdom and obedience to respond to God's will in spirit and truth.

God of the inspired Torah, you have given the gift of your Spirit to renew my mind and convert my heart so that I can discern your will. Help me to seek justice, to love tenderly, and to walk humbly with you.

Continue to pray as the Scriptures swirl within your mind and heart . . .

Contemplatio

Spend some extended silent time asking God to give you the experience of humble gratitude for these many women of the Torah. Ask God to work within your heart, stirring you to make a difference in your family, neighborhood, church, and society.

Write a few words to conclude your time of peaceful contemplation.

Operatio

How has this study of the women of the Torah shaped and changed me? What do I most want to remember and incorporate into my life?

Ancient-Future Bible
Study for Small Groups

A small group for *collatio*, the communal practice of lectio divina, is a wonderful way to let the power of Scripture more deeply nourish participants. Through the thoughts, reflections, prayers, and experiences of the other members of the group, each individual comes to understand Scripture more intensely and experience it more profoundly. By sharing our understanding and wisdom in a faith-filled group of people, we discover how to let God live in every dimension of our lives and we enrich the lives of others.

These groups may be formed in any number of ways, just as you create groups for other learning experiences within your community. Groups composed of no more than a dozen people are best for this experience. It is preferable to give people with various needs a variety of days and times from which to choose.

Small groups are best formed when people are encouraged and supported by a church's pastoral leadership and personally welcomed into these small communities. Personally directed invitations are most effective for convincing people to add another dimension to their schedules.

The collatio should never take the place of one's regular, personal lectio divina. Rather, a weekly communal practice is an ideal extension and continuation of personal, daily sacred reading. At each group session, participants discuss the fruits of their individual lectio divina and practice elements of lectio divina together.

Participants should read carefully the opening sections of this book before joining the group. "The Movements of Lectio Divina," "The Essence of

Lectio Divina," and "Your Personal Practice of Ancient-Future Bible Study" would be helpful sections to review throughout the course of the study.

The full weekly collatio group session is designed for about ninety minutes. Those groups with limited time may choose either Part 1 or Part 2 for the group experience. Instructions for each of the collatio groups are provided on the following pages.

Suggestions for Participating in the Group

‡ The spirit of the collatio should be that of a personal conversation, with the members desiring to learn from one another and building each other up. The divine Word is the teacher; the members of the group are all learners.

‡ The group can avoid the distraction of off-topic chatter by sticking to the text, the commentary, and their personal response to the text from the meditatio.

‡ Group members should be careful to give everyone in the group an opportunity to share. When discussing personal thoughts, members should use "I" language and be cautious about giving advice to others. They should listen attentively to the other members of the group so as to learn from their insights and should not worry about trying to cover all the questions in each gathering. They should select only those that seem the most helpful for group discussion.

‡ Dispute, debate, and dogmatic hairsplitting within the group erode its focus and purpose. Opposition and division destroy the supportive bond of the group. The desire of individuals to assert themselves and their own ideas wears down the spirit of the group. In a community setting, it is often wise to "agree to disagree." An inflexible, pedantic attitude blocks the way to a vital and fulfilling understanding of the passage. The Scriptures are the living Word of God, the full meaning of which we can never exhaust.

‡ It is usually helpful to have someone to guide the process of the group. This facilitator directs the discussion, helping the group keep the discussion on time and on track. The facilitator need not be an expert, either in Scripture or in the process of lectio divina, but simply a person with the skills necessary to guide a group. This role may be rotated among members of the group, if desired.

Group Study in Six Sessions

‡ Begin each group session with hospitality and welcome. Name tags are helpful if group members don't know one another. Offer any announcements or instructions before entering the spirit of prayer.

‡ Set the tone and focus the group by saying the gathering prayer together.

‡ Note that the first group session is a bit different from the others because it involves reading and discussing the introduction. After the first group session, all the remaining sessions follow the same format.

‡ The group sessions are in two parts. Part 1 is a discussion of the fruits of the lectio divina that participants completed on their own since the last group session. The most effective question to ask of each chapter is this: "What insight is most significant to you from your reflection on this chapter?" Group members may mention insights they gained in the lectio, meditatio, oratio, contemplatio, or operatio of each chapter.

‡ Part 2 is a session of lectio divina in the group. Leave at least half of the group time for this section. Move through each of the five movements as described in the chapter. Read the text aloud, followed by the commentary. Leave the most time for the more personal questions of the meditatio. Don't worry if you don't complete them all.

‡ Leave sufficient time for the oratio, contemplatio, and operatio. These movements should not be rushed. Gently guide the group from vocal prayer into a period of restful silence. Don't neglect to conclude the lectio divina by mentioning some practical fruits of operatio before dismissing the group into the world of daily discipleship.

‡ Conclude each group session by encouraging participants to complete the lectio divina on their own for the upcoming chapters. Ask them to write their responses to each movement of lectio in their book.

Collatio Group 1

✝ The first group session is a bit different from the others. After offering greetings and introductions, explain the process of Ancient-Future Bible Study. Then set the tone for the group experience by praying together the gathering prayer.

✝ Gathering prayer:

> *Come upon us, Holy Spirit, to enlighten and guide us as we begin this study of the women of the Torah. You have inspired the biblical authors to give to your people a living Word that has the power to convert our hearts and change our lives. Give us a sense of expectation, trusting that you will shine the light of your truth within us. Bless us as we gather with your gifts of wisdom and discernment so that we may listen to the inspired Word and experience its transforming energy.*

✝ Spend the first half of the collatio group reading the introduction to this book and discussing the questions to consider. A volunteer may read each section aloud, and the group will spend a few minutes discussing the questions that follow.

✝ Spend the second half of the group time following the five movements of the lectio divina at the end of the introduction. Read the text aloud, followed by the commentary. Then spend time reflecting and sharing responses to the questions of the meditatio.

✝ When leading into the oratio, pray the prayer aloud, then leave time for additional prayers from the group. When the vocal prayer has receded, lead the group into contemplatio. Help the group to feel comfortable with the quiet and relax in the presence of God. Conclude the lectio divina with the operatio. Share encouragement and commitment to practice lectio divina throughout the week.

✝ Before departing, instruct group members in their practice of lectio divina during the week. Participants should complete the lectio divina for chapters 1–5 for next week. Encourage them to write their responses to each movement of lectio in their book. The lectio divina for chapter 6 will be done together in the group next week.

Collatio Group 2

✢ Gathering prayer:

> *Creator God, you formed man and woman in your own image and gave them the task of ruling in your name as stewards of creation. We are grateful for the freedom and purpose you have given us, and we desire to orient our lives according to your design for human life. Clothe us with your care and guide us in our struggles as we live outside the garden of your plan for us. Forgive our sins and lead us to the fullness of life for which you created us.*

✢ Part 1:
- Having completed the lectio divina for chapters 1–5 during the week, the group members discuss the fruit of their practice for these five chapters. Divide these chapters into equal time allotments so that no chapter is neglected. To provoke personal discussion of each chapter, ask this question: "What insight is most significant to you from your reflection on this chapter?"

✢ Part 2:
- Spend at least the last half of the group time in the full lectio divina of chapter 6. Move through each step according to the instructions provided in the chapter, leaving plenty of time for oratio, contemplatio, and operatio.

✢ Departure:
- Encourage participants to complete the lectio divina for chapters 7–11 before the next collatio group. Ask them to write their responses to each movement of lectio in their book. The lectio divina for chapter 12 will be done together in the group next week.

Collatio Group 3

✝ Gathering prayer:

> *Faithful God, you called our ancestors to live loyally in your covenant through obedient faith. The lives of Sarah and Hagar demonstrate the fidelity of your promises, while the lives of Lot's wife and daughters show how social pressure and isolation can corrupt our integrity. Give me the courage to maintain my faith in you when under pressure, and help me to deepen my commitment to live in your covenant. Guide my life with trust in your promises and hope in the future.*

✝ Part 1:
- Having completed the lectio divina for chapters 7–11 during the week, the group members discuss the fruit of their practice for these five chapters. Divide these chapters into equal time allotments so that no chapter is neglected. To provoke personal discussion of each chapter, ask this question: "What insight is most significant to you from your reflection on this chapter?"

✝ Part 2:
- Spend at least the last half of the group time in the full lectio divina of chapter 12. Move through each step according to the instructions provided in the chapter, leaving plenty of time for oratio, contemplatio, and operatio.

✝ Departure:
- Encourage participants to complete the lectio divina for chapters 13–17 before the next collatio group. Ask them to write their responses to each movement of lectio in their book. The lectio divina for chapter 18 will be done together in the group next week.

Collatio Group 4

✝ Gathering prayer:

> *God of steadfast love, you chose Rebekah, the beautiful mother of Israel, to reveal your favor for the powerless and the outcast. Her selfless generosity, decisive action, and willingness to take extraordinary risks for the sake of her family's future established her as a model for future generations. Continue to show me your faithful care, guiding my decisions as I seek your will. Show me the way into the future and help me to pass on the legacy of faith to the next generation.*

✝ Part 1:
- Having completed the lectio divina for chapters 13–17 during the week, the group members discuss the fruit of their practice for these five chapters. Divide these chapters into equal time allotments so that no chapter is neglected. To provoke personal discussion of each chapter, ask this question: "What insight is most significant to you from your reflection on this chapter?"

✝ Part 2:
- Spend at least the last half of the group time in the full lectio divina of chapter 18. Move through each step according to the instructions provided in the chapter, leaving plenty of time for oratio, contemplatio, and operatio.

✝ Departure:
- Encourage participants to complete the lectio divina for chapters 19–23 before the next collatio group. Ask them to write their responses to each movement of lectio in their book. The lectio divina for chapter 24 will be done together in the group next week.

Collatio Group 5

✝ Gathering prayer:

> *Lord God, you are our help in ages past and our hope for years to come. You blessed Leah and Rachel with unique gifts while their lives were plagued with comparison, competition, and self-contempt. Help me to appreciate my own special blessings and the many ways my life has been graced by you. As you led the families of Leah and Rachel from their bondage into the land of your promises, guide my life as I call to you in need and trust in your assurances to me.*

✝ Part 1:
- Having completed the lectio divina for chapters 19–23 during the week, the group members discuss the fruit of their practice for these five chapters. Divide these chapters into equal time allotments so that no chapter is neglected. The most effective question to ask of each chapter is this: "What is your most important insight from this chapter?"

✝ Part 2:
- Spend at least the last half of the group time in the full lectio divina of chapter 24. Move through each step according to the instructions provided in the chapter, leaving plenty of time for oratio, contemplatio, and operatio.

✝ Departure:
- Encourage participants to complete the lectio divina for chapters 25–29 before the next collatio group. Ask them to write their responses to each movement of lectio in their book. The lectio divina for chapter 30 will be done together in the group next week.

Collatio Group 6

‡ Gathering prayer:

> *God of freedom and life, the women of the Torah developed a passion for justice and a determination to struggle against the political and social forces that threatened their families and their people. Give me the courage to follow in the footsteps of Tamar, the midwives in Egypt, Moses's mother, Zipporah, and Miriam. Help me to be a mediator of your redeeming power by working for justice and human rights.*

‡ Part 1:
  • Having completed the lectio divina for chapters 25–29 during the week, the group members discuss the fruit of their practice for these five chapters. Divide these chapters into equal time allotments so that no chapter is neglected. The most effective question to ask of each chapter is this: "What is your most important insight from this chapter?"

‡ Part 2:
  • Spend at least the last half of the group time in the full lectio divina of chapter 30. Move through each step according to the instructions provided in the chapter, leaving plenty of time for oratio, contemplatio, and operatio.

‡ Departure:
  • Discuss how this Ancient-Future Bible Study has made a difference in the lives of group members and whether the group wishes to study another book in the series. Consult www.brazospress.com/ancient futurebiblestudy for more study options.